THE FOUR
HORSEMEN
OF
RETIREMENT

THE FOUR HORSEMEN OF RETIREMENT

Ways To Confidently Retire By Planning For
Longevity, Inflation, Taxes, And Healthcare

SPENCER L. FORD, CFP®

WEALTH
AUTHORITY
BOOKS

THE FOUR HORSEMEN OF RETIREMENT

Ways To Confidently Retire By Planning For Longevity, Inflation, Taxes, And Healthcare

ISBN 13: 978-1-966168-34-8
Library of Congress Control Number: 2025913319

Designed by Melissa Farr, Back Porch Creatrive, LLC

Wealth Authority Books
2511 WOODLANDS WAY
OCEANSIDE, CA 92054

Wealth Authority Books is an imprint of Indie Books International, Inc.

www.indiebooksintl.com

To my father and mother, Roger and Carolyn Ford,
my brother, Austin Ford, and my wife, Brittany
Ford, and children, Silas and Noa Ford.

Outlined against a blue, gray October sky the Four Horsemen rode again. In dramatic lore they are known as famine, pestilence, destruction, and death.

—GRANTLAND RICE, *New York Herald Tribune,* October 18, 1924, in a literary allusion to the sixth chapter of the biblical book of Revelation

CONTENTS

FOREWORD

A s a husband and father of three boys, I know the importance of investing for retirement. While I was drafted by the Tennessee Titans in the fourth round of the 2002 NFL Draft, that was not the beginning of my football career. It started when I was seven years old, putting in countless hours of work and preparation, hoping the payoff—a college football scholarship and professional career—would happen sometime in the not-too-distant future.

I believe retirement planning is similar: to have a successful retirement, you want to develop an early understanding of it and take the necessary steps now in order to achieve the payoff you desire in the future.

I was privileged to enjoy an eight-year career, and earning a ring with the Colts in Super Bowl XLI was a high honor. But after those eight years, I needed to create a new life for my family and me. Pursuing work in the media and as a professional speaker was logical for me. Serving as a color analyst for ESPN, calling college football games, and cohosting a 3:00 p.m. to 6:00 p.m. show on 700 WLW-AM in Cincinnati has been a great encore career. The goal of setting myself up for the future is still in play.

As a lifelong Notre Dame fan and eventual captain of the University of Notre Dame football team, I was very much familiar with the football lore of Knute Rockne's 1924 Four Horsemen. This book introduced me to a different way of looking at the four horsemen: the four horsemen of retirement, which include longevity, inflation, taxes, and healthcare. These horsemen stick together in a herd, each assisting their fellow riders. I believe this can be a significant problem for planning for a winning retirement.

The author, Spencer Ford, suggests this is a fixable problem. This book explains the inner workings of life expectancy, inflation, taxation, and some of the potentially obscure costs of healthcare. I hope you enjoy learning about the four horsemen of retirement. Many retirees fail to properly avoid these dilemmas. With the proper game plan, you can be ready to create the retirement you have always dreamed of. That preparation needs to start now.

Rocky Boiman

THE ONE

Dear Reader:

Ed Mylett, the author of #*Maxout Your Life* and *The Power of One More*, talks about the power of "The One." "The One" is that person in a family who makes all the difference. They step up and answer the call—through an act of nature, a keen sense of awareness, the grace of God—or some combination of all three.

Often, it means choosing to live a life contrary to what others may think their circumstances would predict. "The One" often breaks a cycle of poverty, abuse, and violence. They make the conscious decision to create more for themselves and, ultimately, their family.

For my family, "The One" is my father, Roger Ford. He grew up in Steubenville, Ohio, with an abusive father and drug abuse surrounding him. Instead of perpetuating the cycle, he chose to break it. After graduating from high school, he sold plasma and worked nights to put himself through college. He wasn't going to let where he came from determine where he was going.

"The One" does not come out of these circumstances without guides along the way—people who see something in them and show glimmers of hope for a better path. My dad was no exception. Wanting to honor his childhood mentors who showed him this better path, his overwhelming desire became to live a life of service to others.

His initial goal was to become a medical doctor, but the cost of medical school and other factors, such as needing to provide financial support for his younger sister, prevented him from making that a reality. Not one to throw in the towel at the first sign of adversity, he found another passion— helping families create better lives for themselves through their finances. This led him to found Conservative Financial Solutions LLC in 1985.

Today, my brother, Austin Ford, and I get to continue his legacy as owners and co-CEOs of the firm. What we carry on is much more than a business. It is the legacy of "The One," and how we can honor him by building on that legacy.

If ever you see me, please don't hesitate to come up and say hello. Even if I never have the pleasure of meeting you in person, I hope you enjoy this book, and I wish you all the best in overcoming the four horsemen of retirement.

Sincerely,
Spencer Ford, CFP®

PART I

The Horseman
Of Longevity

Chapter One

WHY WORRY ABOUT
THE FOUR HORSEMEN

Y ou may have heard of the four horsemen of the apocalypse, written about by John in the book of Revelation. Those horsemen include conflict, war, famine, and death, sent out to wreak havoc on the world before the final coming of Christ. Whatever your religious affiliation, the four horsemen denote dire consequences. That's the kind of urgency I want to communicate with what I have deemed the four horsemen of retirement—four of the largest hurdles that many retirees face: longevity, inflation, taxes, and healthcare. These horsemen also tend to stick together in a herd, each helping their fellow riders.

How can you prepare yourself to help avoid the potential negative consequences these horsemen represent, separately and collectively? We will discuss each horseman in sequence, highlighting the unique challenges they present while also considering how they often work in tandem with one another. Rather than just simply explaining how to overcome them, I also want to dive into the background of each rider. Recognizing the nature of each rider, what contributes to their power, and how they might work together will provide a deeper understanding of the issues they pose, and, ultimately, it will contribute to the knowledge of how to help you surmount them as well.

One caveat: the goal is not necessarily to defeat the horsemen. The goal is to conquer the dilemmas they present. Some horsemen you cannot defeat no matter what you do. Others, longevity, in particular, you do not want to beat. You do want to be able to prevail over the challenges of longevity and the obstacles the other horsemen represent. Even though you cannot defeat the horsemen, you can overcome them, and that is what you are truly after in retirement.

I believe that longevity is perhaps the most pervasive of all the horsemen and may have the greatest impact on the other horsemen, so we will look at longevity first.

Where Does The Idea Of Retirement Come From?

Let's begin at the beginning.

Some of the earliest records for the concept of retirement date back to the time of the Roman Empire. Records show that in 13 BC, Emperor Augustus initiated a program that would pay soldiers who had served for twenty years in the military an ongoing income from the state. This was done to keep older soldiers, who were replaced by younger soldiers, from revolting against the empire.[1] Since then, the concept of retirement has continued to evolve.

Despite its origin dating back to ancient Rome, the concept of retirement as it exists today is a new phenomenon. The remaining life expectancy in ancient Rome, if you had the good fortune to make it to adulthood, was around the age of fifty.[2] German Chancellor Otto von Bismarck created Europe's first modern welfare state by establishing old-age pensions sponsored by the state in 1889.[3] Bismarck enacted this program to stave off a revolt by encouraging citizens aged seventy and older to leave the workforce voluntarily to create room for younger, unemployed Germans. Bismarck is quoted as saying, "Those who are disabled from work by age and invalidity have a well-grounded claim to care from the state."[4] It would not be until the depths of the Great Depression in the 1930s that the United States developed the Social Security program.

In the 1800s, if you were fortunate enough to make it to adulthood, life expectancy tapped out around age sixty.[5] It wasn't until the twentieth century that we started to see dramatic rises in life expectancy, mainly due to improvements in sanitation, housing, education, and medicine.[6] Now, the average American who makes it to adulthood can expect to live to age seventy-eight,[7,8] a life span 56 percent longer than our Roman predecessors. If you make it to age sixty-five, you can expect to live to an average age of eighty-three,[9] but even that is a little misleading.

According to the Society of Actuaries, there is a 50 percent chance that for a married couple, each aged sixty-five today, one spouse will be alive at ninety-two.[10] Another thing to consider is the fact that these life expectancy tables account for risk factors that not everyone has. If you exercise regularly, are a nonsmoker, and assess yourself to be in good or excellent health, your life expectancy is anywhere from two to three years longer than the average. It's no wonder that 49 percent of pre-retirees underestimate their life expectancy by five or more years.[11]

The concept of retiring and expecting to live for another twenty-five to thirty years has existed for less than a century. In the context of human history, this new state of life, known as retirement, is in its infancy. It's no wonder that many are still trying to figure it out. For most, twenty-five to thirty years is the longest stretch of unemployment they have ever faced, and it comes with unique challenges. My aim is to address what is commonly identified as the four largest hurdles retirees face and provide a guide to help you overcome the four horsemen of retirement: longevity, inflation, taxes, and healthcare.

Forging My Own Path

Before you take a guided tour of the four horsemen of retirement, I thought it would be a good idea for you to meet the tour guide.

Raising his five children, my father never tried to persuade any of us to go into the family business. He would always say, "Do what you love, and the money will come." If he attempted to persuade us to do anything, it was to carve our own path. Despite this, I always found myself involved in the business at a young age. Growing up, I never idolized athletes, movie stars, or musicians. I've never asked for an autograph. My father has always been my hero, so as a young child, I was in awe of the family business.

My father didn't believe in paying us an allowance. Chores—like taking out the trash, cleaning up, and taking care of the animals on our little farm—were part of being in the family. You didn't get paid for those things. That's just what loving families do for each other. But he was happy to pay us to help with the business.

From the time I was five years old, I remember cleaning off the kitchen table with my siblings after a family dinner so we could stuff envelopes together to mail out invitations for an upcoming financial workshop my father was conducting. As I got older, I started setting up and tearing down those workshops for my father. Later those nights, back at home, I would recite the workshop from memory to my mother, making sure to mimic my father's cadence, motions, and even the timing of the jokes he told. In elementary school, if you asked me what I was going to be when I grew up, I would tell you that I was going to be a financial advisor just like my father.

Things changed for me when I entered high school, as they do for most adolescents. I had a short rebellious stage but really connected with one of my youth ministers. Knowing I wanted to live a life in service to others as my father did, but not wanting to blindly follow in his footsteps, I decided to go into full-time ministry. After high school, I attended Cincinnati Christian University to obtain my bachelor of arts in biblical studies. At this point, I was already the junior high youth minister for my church.

After my undergraduate studies, I decided to further my education by earning a master's degree in counseling with the goal of becoming better equipped to help others. To become licensed as a counselor, I had to complete a certain number of clinical hours under supervision after graduating. This led to me becoming the lead therapist at a residential unit at a local hospital. To qualify to be a resident in the program, clients had to have both a severe mental illness and a severe drug addiction. If the residents failed the program, they went to jail, so the motives of the residents were questionable at best. Looking back at it now, it was a program that wasn't particularly built for success.

As you might imagine, the burnout rate for the staff working with the type of population we were working with is significant. I poured my heart and soul into this job. Often, on my days off, I would swing by the unit to grab some of the residents so we could get breakfast together or go to the local community center. Regardless of my efforts, the failure rate was high. It wasn't so much about helping someone learn how to live a better life as much as it was trying to help them stay alive another week.

Things came to a head for me in the fall of 2015. I was set to get married the following year. I really started to think hard about the type of husband and father I ultimately wanted to be and become for my wife and family, as well as the type of lifestyle I wanted to provide. As I was mulling this over in my mind, as fate would have it, an incident occurred on the unit. A client I was counseling was on a mandatory seventy-two-hour hold and suicide watch. As I was often on call, I came in to see the patient, who was experiencing a breakdown. The patient became violent; somehow, he had gotten drugs into the facility and was now going through withdrawal. He physically lashed out, and to escape the facility, he pulled the fire alarm and fled. I never saw him again.

I had a career where I was helping people but not making the impact on people's lives that I wanted to, and I knew I could. I expressed this frustration to my hero and mentor, my father.

My image as a child of what a financial advisor did was sitting behind a closed door all day, punching a calculator. I didn't want to do that. I wanted to be directly involved with helping others. But now my father told me story upon story of all the families he had helped throughout the years, the life-changing differences he was able to help families create through their finances. Through our talks, my father quickly changed my perspective, and I once again felt that pull to the financial industry that I felt when I was young.

My father, being on the tail end of the baby boomer generation, holds to the mindset that things must be earned, not given. I wasn't going to just waltz my way into the family business due to nepotism. If I was serious, I was going to have to earn it, so I got to work. I started by studying for and passing my insurance exam. After that, I studied and passed my securities exam in under three weeks, reading solely from a training manual and with no prior knowledge. That was enough to get my father's attention, and he brought me into the business in January 2016.

Shortly after that, I enrolled in the financial planning program at Ohio State University, which eventually allowed me to sit for the Certified Financial Planner™ (CFP®) exam. Like I said, there's no tolerance for doing things halfway in my family. To earn my credentials as a CFP, which holds itself out there as being the highest financial planning designation one can achieve, not only did I have to pass the exam, but much like my counseling license, I had to complete a certain number of hours under supervision. For the CFP, it's three thousand hours. As of now, I currently hold three separate securities licenses (Series 7, 63, and 65), my insurance license, and the CFP® designation.

It's funny; through a roundabout way, I finished where I had started, in the financial planning industry, helping others achieve their financial goals and dreams, and I couldn't be happier. It's an honor, privilege, and enormous responsibility for my brother Austin and I to continue the legacy my father started. We honor the heroic efforts of "The One" for our family, not just for our family but for all the families we are blessed to serve, to help not only create wealth in this generation but for generations to come. When Austin and I purchased Conservative Financial Solutions LLC in 2022, we wanted to create a vision for the company that we felt fully encompassed our mission. That vision is for Conservative Financial Solutions to be the leader in helping families make informed financial decisions so they can live longer, happier, and more fulfilling lives. It's my desire that this book helps you on that journey.

My aim is to help people plan for a long life, one where they do not run out of money. Let's explore that notion in the following chapter.

Chapter Two

PLANNING FOR A LONG LIFE

The quality, not the longevity,
of one's life is what is important.[12]
Rev. Martin Luther King Jr.

I t is cliché to even mention it at this point, but it remains true. The number one concern of many retirees is not having enough money for retirement and thus running the risk of running out of money before running out of life.[13] Not only that, but they worry about running out of money more than they fear death.[14]

All the horsemen work together, but none has as much influence on the others as longevity. The longer you live, the more powerful the other horsemen become, and the more planning must take place to help you overcome them, which is why it makes sense to start with longevity.

A long life is a blessing. However, not preparing properly for longevity can be devastating to retirement. This is a prime example of how the four horsemen of retirement work together. Longevity can mean running out of money before you run out of life, succumbing to the potential effects of inflation, paying more in taxes, and seeing your hard-earned savings significantly reduced by exorbitant healthcare costs toward the end of life.

All these risks could be mitigated through proper planning.

It is no secret that, overall, we are living longer. In 1940, the first year that Social Security started passing out monthly checks,[15] the average male who made it to age sixty-five was expected to live to age seventy-eight, and the average female was expected to live to age eighty.[16] Today, a male who makes it to age sixty-five is expected to live to age eighty-two, and a female is expected to live to age eighty-five,[17] but the story does not end there. As noted in the previous chapter, there is a 50 percent chance that for a married couple age sixty-five today, one spouse will be alive at ninety-two; life expectancy tables account for risk factors that don't apply to everyone, and as stated before, almost half of retirees underestimate their life expectancy by at least five years. It should not come as a surprise that living an extra five years than what was expected can be financially damaging for those who are not adequately prepared for such a scenario.

Underestimating life expectancy is not something you want to do. A great way to anticipate the potential effects of this obstacle is to tack on an extra five years to your retirement plan and see how well it holds up.

The average age at which people retire in the United States is sixty-three.[18] As we discussed, the average life expectancy at age sixty-five is anywhere between eighty-three and eighty-six. That equates to twenty to twenty-three years in retirement. That is twenty to twenty-three years of unemployment. For most retirees, retirement is the longest period of unemployment they will face in their lifetime. Think about that for a moment. Has there ever been a period when you have been unemployed for over twenty years? Most of us have our first job as teenagers, and we do everything we can to avoid stretches of unemployment after that.

The way you address the horseman of longevity is by successfully mitigating the other three horsemen. While I believe that no horseman has a greater effect on retirement than longevity, it will take the taming of the other three—inflation, taxes, and healthcare—to subdue it. If you can successfully mitigate the horsemen of inflation, taxes, and healthcare, the effects of the horseman of longevity may even be turned in your favor. In other words, a longer life could lead to even more financial prosperity.

With all this in mind, let's learn ways to help you overcome the horseman of inflation to make a long and happy retirement a reality.

PART II

The Horseman
Of Inflation

Chapter Three

HOW WE GOT HERE

*The important next step is to recognize that today,
governments control the quantity of money.
So that as a result, inflation in the United States
is made in Washington and nowhere else.*[19]
Milton Friedman

O n April 5, 1933, President Franklin D. Roosevelt initiated the first step in removing the dollar from the gold standard through an executive order that dictated to all United States citizens that all gold coins and gold certificates in denominations of more than one hundred dollars be turned into the Federal Reserve by May 1 in exchange for dollars.[20]

Up to this point, the gold standard as a monetary system directly linked the country's currency to the value of gold. A fixed price and amount of gold made it so the country could not arbitrarily create more money than could be redeemed in gold. The physical quantity of gold acted as a limit to issuance, making sure the government could not simply create more money out of thin air. This system was used to create price stability and avoid the evils of inflation.[21]

President Nixon put the final nail in the coffin of the United States gold standard on August 15, 1971, when he announced that the United States would no longer convert dollars to gold at a fixed value. With this, the only thing backing the dollar was the full faith and credit of the United States government and its citizens. There was no longer any concrete, tangible underlying asset like gold that the value of the US dollar was tied to, therefore providing the path for the government to print as many dollars as it sees fit. It did not take long after that for inflation to rear its ugly head. Three years later, in 1974, inflation reached 11.05 percent before peaking in 1980 at 13.55 percent.[22]

Attempting to fight inflation and pass the responsibility off to some other entity, Congress modified the original act that had created the Federal Reserve (Fed) with the passing of the Federal Reserve Reform Act of 1977. In the act, Congress lays out what is now known as the dual mandate for the Fed. The act reads as follows:

> *The Board of Governors of the Federal Reserve System and the Federal Open Market Committee shall maintain long run growth of the monetary and credit aggregates commensurate with the economy's long run potential to increase production, so as to promote effectively the goals of maximum employment, stable prices, and moderate long-term interest rates.*[23]

Above, you see the first mandate of the Fed is to maximize employment while the second mandate is to create stable prices and moderate long-term rates. Maximum employment is meant to help the economy continue to move forward through the means of production. More workers in the workforce should translate to increased production. Stable prices and moderate long-term rates provide investors and entrepreneurs with a level of predictability and the confidence to invest in new ventures. How does the Fed fulfill these two mandates? They do it by manipulating the money supply.

Inflation, in simplified terms, is too many dollars chasing too few goods. It is basic supply and demand economics. If the demand increases because everyone has more money, but the supply cannot keep up with demand, prices will increase. That is what happens when a windfall of new money enters the economic system without the support of an increase in the production of goods and services.

When the US dollar was attached to the gold standard, inflation occurred when significant discoveries of new gold were made, such as the California Gold Rush of the 1840s and '50s. New gold meant an increase in the money supply. If that increase was more than the production of new goods and services, inflation was the result. The same type of inflation occurred when John Stewart MacArthur developed the cyanidation process for extracting gold from complex ores in 1887.[24] This development led to an increase in gold, which led to an increase in the money supply, which led to inflation.

Even with the discoveries surrounding gold, the money supply was more stable than printing money out of thin air. There still had to be the physical gold to back up the amount of money that was produced. Once the United States left the gold standard, all bets were off. The Fed, armed with its new mandates by Congress, now had and still has control of the money supply.

However, as Milton Friedman, an American economist and statistician who was awarded the Nobel Prize in economics in 1976, points out, the Fed is not the only one to blame for inflation. They get their marching orders from us, the American people.

The truth is that you and I are the biggest culprits in inflation. As Americans, overall, we consistently ask the government to do the impossible. We want the government to spend someone else's money on us, but not to spend our money on anyone else. What does the government do? The government typically collects trillions of dollars in taxes but spends even more trillions.[25] Who pays the difference? It is not the tooth fairy. It is not Santa Claus. It is you and me. We pay for it through inflation. The government prints the extra trillion dollars it needs by increasing the money supply. The increase in money leads to inflation, and the dollars we are allowed to hold onto after taxes are not worth as much.[26]

In this view, inflation could be viewed like a tax, another one of our horsemen. This is one example of how they ride together and not separately. Inflation is the perfect tax. Congress does not have to vote on it. It just happens, and until the public becomes more aware of how government spending truly affects them, we will continue to repeat cycles of high inflation and experience the continued erosion of our purchasing power.

```
          RECEIPT
- - - - - - - - - - - - - - - - -
½ G Milk   .....................
½ G Orange Juice   ........
TV Dinner   ...................
Bread   .........................
Mac & Cheese   ............
Laundry Detergent   ......
Cling Wrap   .................
Toilet Paper   ...............
Army Men   ...................
Dryer Sheets   .............
- - - - - - - - - - - - - - - - -
TOTAL:            $19.83
       ***Customer Copy ***
          December 1990
```

Inflation is a disease. It's a dangerous disease for a society.
It is sometimes a fatal disease for a society.
It is a disease that, if allowed to rage unchecked,
can destroy a society, and we have many such examples.[27]

Milton Freidman

A Bag Of Groceries

You and I have little control over monetary policy. The question
is, how can we best deal with the reality of inflation? The
costs of goods and services typically rise over time; therefore,
addressing inflation in retirement is of significant importance.
The bag of groceries you buy today for a hundred dollars
could cost $150 in the not-so-distant future.

Do you remember the movie *Home Alone* that came out
in 1990? It is the holiday classic where Kevin McCallister is
accidentally left behind while his family goes on vacation to

Paris for Christmas. In the movie, Kevin goes to the grocery store to pick up some items for his solo staycation.

The grocery list included a half gallon of milk, a half gallon of orange juice, a TV dinner, bread, frozen mac and cheese, laundry detergent, cling wrap, toilet paper, a pack of army men, and dryer sheets. The total is $19.83. In 2023, the same list of items cost $72.28,[28] an increase of 264.5 percent or an average of four percent per year.

Albert Einstein is sometimes attributed with saying, "Compound interest is the eighth wonder of the world. He who understands it, earns it. He who doesn't, pays it." We'll talk about the beneficial power of compound interest as it relates to your investments, but unfortunately, the powers of compound interest are at work with inflation. The horseman of inflation knows how to wield the power of compound interest, as we can see from McCallister's grocery bill.

Mitigating inflation is necessary for survival. Like we discussed at the beginning of this book, you are not going to defeat the horsemen, but you can reduce their impact. You're not going to beat inflation, but you can better manage it. You cannot beat inflation because the Fed is not trying to completely stop inflation. The Fed's target inflation rate is 2 percent.[29] The Fed wants to keep inflation at 2 percent, not get it to zero, and because of compounding interest, that means that every twenty years, your dollars are going to purchase roughly 50 percent less than what they purchased before. Essentially, your dollar today could be worth fifty cents twenty years from now. This is why it is necessary to reduce the effects of inflation as much as possible.

In recent years, we would all welcome inflation of only 2 percent. In 2021, the US inflation rate was 4.7 percent, in 2022, it was 8 percent, in 2023, it was 4.1 percent, and in 2024 it was 3.2 percent.[30] That means that a bag of groceries that cost one hundred dollars at the beginning of 2021 would cost $121 by the end of 2024. That is an increase of 21 percent. Said another way, if you had one hundred dollars at the beginning of 2021, its purchasing power was only seventy-nine dollars in 2024.[31] That is a rapid decline in the value of your money, which makes having a path to help overcome inflation that much more important.

Inflation And The Bane Of Bracket Creep

As you can see, the horseman of inflation comes at you from multiple angles, making goods cost more and the value of your dollar less. And, yes, inflation is similar to a tax, a tax that hits you twice. Here's what I mean: Not only does inflation decrease your purchasing power, but each year, the Internal Revenue Service (IRS) adjusts the tax brackets for inflation. How is that a tax? After all, you may be receiving more money, but your purchasing power has declined. What you pay in taxes should reflect that. The problem is that those brackets are expanded based on what is known as the chained consumer price index (C-CPI), not the consumer price index (CPI). Who cares? You should. Here is a quote straight from the Congressional Budget Office: "The chained consumer price index for all urban consumers (CPI-U) results in lower estimates of inflation than the traditional CPI does."[32]

This means that while the rate of inflation expands, your tax bracket does not expand enough to keep up, creating a situation called bracket creep. As journalist Julia Keagan describes it, "Bracket creep occurs when inflation pushes individuals into higher tax brackets. The result is an increase in income taxes but no increase in real purchasing power."[33]

If you get a raise during times of inflation, congratulations, you have more money. It doesn't buy as much, and the government could then take more of it from you. To add insult to injury, these tax inflation adjustments are always a year behind. Tax brackets for the year are decided in the previous year. Therefore, they cannot account for inflation in the current year. A great illustration of this is what happened in 2022. The tax brackets for 2022 were decided in 2021. Year-over-year inflation was 8%, and as of September 2022, it was 8.2 percent,[34] yet the 2022 brackets were only expanded by a little over 3 percent.[35] This can create an environment for bracket creep to move even faster.

To learn more about inflation, please visit thefourhorsemenbook.com.

Chapter Four

INFLATION

For many retirees today, the traditional three-legged stool is broken.

In earlier days of financial planning, practitioners would talk about the three-legged stool of retirement: Social Security, personal savings, and pensions.

Back when this image was widely used, each income source provided balanced support to a successful retirement income plan.

THE THREE-LEGGED STOOL THAT *WAS*

Pension

Social Security

Personal Savings

Today, the three-legged stool doesn't exist the way it used to. It looks more like this figure.

THE THREE-LEGGED STOOL THAT *IS*

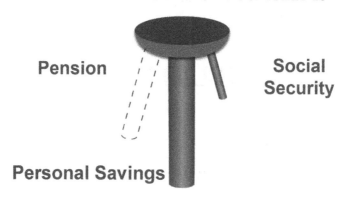

Pension

Social Security

Personal Savings

What has changed? A lot. First, as you can see, the Social Security leg has shrunk significantly. That's because Social Security doesn't provide the support that it once did. We will discuss why that is in chapters 5 and 6.

The pension leg is not only shrinking, but it is nonexistent for most retirees in the private sector. In fact, while many public sector workers may have a pension, private-sector workers are about two-thirds less likely to have a pension than in the middle to the end of the 1970s.[36,37] As with Social Security, those who do retire with a pension will see that leg continue to shrink in the support it provides over time.

These days, the most important, most outsized leg of the stool is typically personal savings. Much of your success in retirement is going to come down to how effectively you can use your personal savings to provide for you in retirement.

The strength of your retirement income depends in part on your ability to mitigate inflation and the rest of the four horsemen. The ability of your retirement plan to continue to produce more income for you each year to keep up with inflation and even surpass it is key. We will tackle each income source in the following chapters, starting with Social Security.

Chapter Five

SOCIAL SECURITY

The first question I always get when it comes to Social Security is, "Will it even be around for me when I retire?" This is the elephant in the room with Social Security. What many people don't know is that while the program is underfunded, even when the trust fund runs out, the resources exist to pay out seventy-nine cents on the dollar, assuming Congress does nothing in the coming decade to shore it up.[38,39] That is not great news, but seventy-nine cents is notably not zero. And since the disengagement from the gold standard, we know the government "finds" money when it wants to. Social Security is going to continue to exist in some form, but to be sustainable long term, it is going to need some changes.

According to the Center on Budget and Policy Priorities, 97 percent of older adults (aged sixty to eighty-nine) in the United States either receive or will receive Social Security in their lifetime.[40]

Choosing when to start taking Social Security will have a lasting impact on your retirement and your ability to mitigate inflation. Social Security by itself will not be enough to effectively mitigate inflation. The challenge is how you integrate Social Security with what you have personally saved. The "when" of Social Security needs to be part of your overall plan for addressing the horseman of inflation.

At the end of the day, when to start drawing Social Security is a personal decision and unique to each individual and family. In fact, if you call the Social Security Administration, a representative is not permitted to guide you on when you should take Social Security. They can answer questions. They can tell you what you are allowed and not allowed to do, but they cannot guide you to any specific conclusion.

No financial advisor can make the decision for you, either, but working with someone who understands the rules and regulations of Social Security can benefit you tremendously in the decision-making process. You essentially get one chance to get it right when it comes to starting your Social Security, and there are a lot of factors to consider. We will discuss several of those factors, along with how Social Security might best be integrated into an overall financial plan to help you mitigate inflation and the other horsemen, but first, we will discuss why Social Security is not likely to keep up with inflation from the start.

It is true that Social Security provides cost-of-living adjustments (COLAs), but Social Security will still struggle to keep up with inflation in a meaningful way for several reasons. Similar to the tax brackets, the increase for Social Security is decided in the previous year. Sure, Social Security recipients received a COLA of 8.7 percent for 2023, but that was for inflation that happened in 2022. If you couple lagging

COLAs with taxes on Social Security, which we will discuss when we get the horseman of taxes, it is no wonder that the purchasing power of your Social Security check will decline over time.

Based on an ongoing study conducted by the Senior Citizens League, Social Security benefits have lost 40 percent of their buying power since 2000.[41] Even with the cost-of-living adjustments, a dollar of Social Security in 2000 is worth sixty cents today. The bracket creep issue also affects your Social Security if you have not already made that connection.

There is a large issue lurking concerning Social Security as well, and it is no secret. Social Security is underfunded, and according to the 2024 *Annual Report of the Board of Trustees of the Federal Old-Age and Survivors Insurance and Federal Disability Insurance Trust Funds*, the trust fund will be depleted by 2035. At that point, continuing program income will be sufficient to pay 79 percent of scheduled benefits. Needless to say, a potential reduction in Social Security benefits is not going to bode well in the battle to keep up with inflation, and there is speculation that the large COLA increases we have seen in recent years may expedite the projected insolvency date.[42]

Here's the silver lining. According to the Pew Research Center, a majority of all registered voters (52 percent) are aged fifty and older.[43] Why is that important? Well, it will take an act of Congress to make changes to entitlement programs like Social Security and Medicare, and what does every politician want more than anything else? Your vote, so the great speculation by many legislative analysts is that changes will need to be made to Social Security in order to make it sustainable, but the likely scenario is that those age fifty-five and older will be grandfathered into the current version of Social Security.[44] That is by no means a guarantee, but at least there seems to be some reason to believe that those closest to retirement will receive the benefit they were promised. If you are under fifty-five, it's best to plan that Social Security may look notably different than it did for your parents.

Social Security alone will likely not keep up with inflation, given its previous track record, and its level of underfunding is concerning, to say the least. Those reasons alone make it so important to ensure you are maximizing your benefit and properly integrating Social Security into your overall plan. Combine that with the fact that Social Security is estimated to replace 39 percent[45] of the average retiree's income, and it is hard to overstate the importance of getting Social Security right. The confines of this book will not allow us to cover all the angles when it comes to considering how or when you should take Social Security, so let me reemphasize the importance of seeking the help of a financial professional who understands the Social Security system and how it functions, so he or she can help you integrate Social Security into your unique financial plan. The integration of Social Security into your overall financial plan is key.

When To Start Drawing Social Security

At this writing, one can technically start drawing from Social Security as early as age sixty-two. But when *should* you start? Before making that decision, here are a few things you should know.

Your Social Security benefit is calculated using two factors: your earnings record and your full retirement age. Your earnings record is based on your highest thirty-five years of earnings. A mathematical indexing formula is used to figure out your monthly average for those years. If you don't have thirty-five years of earnings, a zero will be counted for each year until the calculation includes thirty-five years. For example, if you only have thirty years of earnings, you will also have five years of zeros to get to thirty-five. If you have forty years of earnings, only your highest thirty-five years of earnings are included in the calculation.

Your full retirement age is the age you can collect Social Security without a reduction for starting early. To check your full retirement age, check the figure below.[46]

Social Security Full Retirement Age	
Year Of Birth	Full Retirement Age
1943–1954	66
1955	66 and 2 months
1956	'66 and 4 months
1957	6 and 6 months
1958	66 and 8 months
1959	66 and 10 months
1960+	67

For most Americans, their full retirement age is sixty-seven, so we will use that for our examples.

The earliest age you can start drawing Social Security is age sixty-two, but as alluded to above, there is a penalty for starting early. Your benefit is reduced by 5 percent or more for each year you start drawing Social Security prior to your full retirement age. If your full retirement age is sixty-seven, and you start drawing Social Security at age sixty-two, it is a permanent reduction of 30 percent to your monthly benefit. If your monthly benefit was going to be $2,500 a month at age sixty-seven, at age sixty-two, the benefit would be reduced to $1,750 a month for life. That's significant, especially in the fight to keep up with inflation. It is hard to lock in a loss of 30 percent off the top and still expect to overcome the rate of inflation.

To really bring this to light, we need to bring the horseman of longevity back into the conversation. Suppose you expect to live to age ninety. Using the figures above, if you waited until your full retirement age to start drawing Social Security as opposed to starting early, you would receive $102,000 more from Social Security over your lifetime.

If you delay drawing Social Security beyond your full retirement age, under current law, you will receive an 8 percent simple interest increase to your benefit each year that you delay until age seventy, for a maximum increase to your benefit of 24 percent.

There is no reason to delay drawing Social Security past age seventy because there is no benefit in doing so. You no longer get any kind of increase for delaying, so go ahead and take it. Continuing our example, based on a full retirement age benefit of $2,500 a month at sixty-seven, at age seventy, upon receiving the 8 percent interest increase each year, your benefit would be $3,100 a month for the rest of your life. Had you waited until age seventy to collect Social Security instead of starting at age sixty-two, you would—if you lived to age ninety—receive an additional $156,000 of benefits over your lifetime.

An important caveat: These examples do not include the cost-of-living adjustments that Social Security provides. Since 2000, Social Security cost-of-living adjustments have averaged 2.58 percent per year.[47] If we add that into the equations above, waiting until your full retirement age to collect Social Security instead of taking it at sixty-two results in an additional $204,997 over your lifetime, up from $102,000. Waiting until age seventy results in an additional $327,370 above taking it at age sixty-two, up from $156,000. Creating additional income of tens or potentially hundreds of thousands of dollars in retirement by just taking Social Security at the right time can make a significant difference when it comes to your fight against inflation.

Run The Numbers And Choose What Makes Sense For You

When you start drawing Social Security early, such as at age sixty-two, you are not just receiving a penalty from the Social Security Administration for early collection. You have locked yourself into an inflationary penalty as well. A 2.58 percent COLA compounded on a reduced amount (for starting to draw at age sixty-two) equates to a lot less dollars added over time than a 2.58 percent COLA compounded on your full retirement age amount, even though you have to wait an additional five years to collect from age sixty-two to sixty-seven. Just like taxes, with Social Security, some people make the mistake of only recognizing the dollars that are physically entering or leaving their pockets. They do not take into consideration the invisible hand of inflation.

Now, let's take a giant step back. I'm not advocating that everyone waits until age seventy or even their full retirement age to take Social Security. I am advocating that you run your numbers. According to a study by United Income, only 4 percent of retirees start claiming their Social Security benefits at the most financially optimal time—only 4 percent.[48] The remaining 96 percent of retirees are losing out on a collective $3.4 trillion in potential retirement income. That's approximately $111,000 per household.[49]

Imagine you had a time machine and used it to start claiming your Social Security in different ways and at different times. Once you have started your benefit, you can travel to the future to see which strategy is right for you. Time machines don't exist (yet), but good financial planning and running the numbers in many ways can help you see potential future outcomes.

There are plenty of solid programs out there that allow you, or a financial professional, to plug in your numbers and multiple scenarios to show which strategy is right for you. Keep in mind that the software is only as good as the data it is working with. Inputting bad data is going to give you bad information: garbage in, garbage out.

Running your numbers will allow you to integrate Social Security into your financial plan properly. It also allows you to find out what your crossover age is. Your crossover age, also referred to as the "breakeven" age, is the age in which waiting would have made more sense than taking early. Typically, the crossover age for someone waiting until age sixty-seven (full retirement age for anyone born 1960 or later) versus taking it at age sixty-two is between seventy-six and eighty years of age. Again, tomorrow isn't promised today, but as we have seen, the difference between starting to draw your Social Security early instead of waiting can be substantial. Plus, delaying the start of drawing Social Security does not have to mean delaying the start of your retirement.

Chapter Six

INTEGRATING SOCIAL SECURITY INTO YOUR FINANCIAL PLAN

L et's look at a hypothetical example of integrating Social Security into a financial plan. For purposes of this illustration, we'll assume I sat down with a family for a discovery visit. This is the first step in the 3D retirement process, which you can learn more about in the final chapter. This is the initial visit where we discuss plans, goals, and values to see if a person's or family's situation is a good fit for our firm. I always ask during the visit if they have a plan for starting to claim Social Security. Our hypothetical couple for this visit happened to be with a married couple, Steve and Linda.[50]

Steve is a big guy with an even bigger personality. When he walks into a room, people gravitate toward him. When I asked Steve and Linda if they had already thought about when they wanted to begin claiming Social Security, Steve informed me that he was absolutely beginning to withdraw

Social Security as soon as he turned sixty-two. Curious, I asked why.

Steve's reasons were that he had been paying into Social Security his whole life, and it was about time the government started paying him back. He had concerns about his Social Security benefit being reduced in the future because of underfunding and wanted to ensure that he was at least going to get something out of the program before that happened. Lastly, he mentioned that he didn't know if he was going to live to his full retirement age. There is validity to everything Steve had to say.

Steve got his first job, busing tables at a restaurant when he was fourteen. That is when he started paying into Social Security. As I've already mentioned, when one chooses to take Social Security is an individual choice, but let's look a little deeper into Steve's reasons.

Since age fourteen, Steve has, in his words, been working his whole life. He wanted the government to start paying him back what it owed him. It's hard to argue against that, but if Steve starts Social Security at sixty-two, the government is paying him back at a 30 percent reduction. As we have seen from previous examples, Steve is doing the government a favor by starting at sixty-two. Social Security is underfunded, but benefits aren't expected to be zero. Even if benefits do get reduced in the future, does anyone want to receive a reduction on top of an already 30 percent reduction? Lastly, tomorrow isn't promised today, but there is nothing in Steve's family medical history that indicates he won't live past his full retirement age of sixty-seven or even his crossover age if he were to delay taking Social Security. In fact, earlier in the visit, he indicated that, based on his personal and family history, he believed his life expectancy to be in his late eighties. It's not an easy decision, but often, it makes more sense to plan for what is most likely to happen than all the what-ifs life can throw at us.

Even with a potential 30 percent reduction for starting early, age sixty-two is still far and away, one of the most popular ages to start drawing Social Security.[51] With no guarantees about the future, some choose to start as soon as they are eligible.

Beyond Steve's reasons, perhaps the biggest reason why age sixty-two is such a popular age to start drawing Social Security has to do with the fact that the average retirement age in the United States is sixty-three.[52] The natural inclination for many is to have the start of withdrawing Social Security coincide with retirement so that Social Security can replace a portion of the income they are leaving behind. That seems logical enough. Yet there is no mandate that states you must start drawing Social Security at retirement. It is often the case that even if you retire, it may be advantageous to still delay drawing Social Security for a time to get a larger benefit.

Retire, but wait on drawing Social Security? That may seem counterintuitive at first. Most retirees absolutely need Social Security to make it in retirement. They simply have not saved enough to survive without it if their intent is to maintain the same standard of living they have become accustomed to, but just because you need Social Security to make it in retirement doesn't mean that your best choice is to start it as soon as you retire, for all the reasons we have already gone through.

Beginning to withdraw early means a permanent penalty on your monthly benefit. It means succumbing to a reduction in cost-of-living adjustments on a dollar-for-dollar basis. Both of these can lead to leaving tens or potentially even hundreds of thousands of dollars on the table in Social Security benefits throughout your lifetime, so what is the alternative?

The alternative is having a financial plan that approximates the optimal time for you to start taking Social Security by integrating as many aspects of your family's financial life as possible. It is difficult to get the timing right for when to begin taking Social Security without looking at the whole picture. It's great to know your crossover age, but that can't be the only basis on which you make the decision on when to take Social Security.

No financial decision should be made in a vacuum. Every financial decision is like a row of dominoes. When you push one domino over, there is another that is sure to follow. That is inevitable, and it isn't inherently a bad thing. There are unintended and intended chain reactions. You must make financial decisions; you just don't want to be surprised by how those decisions may affect other areas of your financial life. This conversation will become relevant again when discussing taxes.

For Steve and Linda, it turned out—as is often the case—that even after retiring, they would benefit from delaying Social Security withdrawals until their full retirement age. For them, that meant pulling extra from their retirement savings during the first several years of retirement to replace their income.

Fortunately, they had enough built up in retirement assets to sustain this strategy, and once they started drawing Social

Security at their full benefit, they could dramatically reduce the income they needed to draw from their investments.

This strategy, according to the hypothetical figures, increased their projected retirement success probability by 10 percent and added a possible $264,597 to their retirement savings. It's important to note that these figures are based on a fictional example and actual results can vary widely.

Other Factors For Social Security

There are a whole host of other planning factors when it comes to Social Security, such as benefits for spouses, widows, and divorced spouses. If you plan to work while taking Social Security, there are factors to consider, too. You even have to consider the taxes that you may have to pay on your Social Security benefit. We will cover taxes as it relates to Social Security when we discuss the horseman of taxes, but as for the other topics, there isn't enough room in the confines of this book. However, you should know that the way your spouse takes Social Security could, in fact, affect your future benefit, so for more resources on Social Security, please visit thefourhorsemenbook.com.

Chapter Seven

PENSIONS

Fun fact: American Express Company implemented the first employer-provided pension plan in the United States in 1875. From that point in time until the creation of the 401(k) plan in 1978, the popularity of pension plans exploded in the United States.

Between 1978 and today, the use of pensions in corporate America has declined dramatically. Public school teachers, nurses, union workers, and state and local government workers are most likely to still have pensions as part of their benefits packages. If you won't be receiving a pension in retirement, please feel free to skip to chapter 8.

Just like Social Security isn't going to save you from the horseman of inflation, neither is your pension, and for similar reasons. Also, like Social Security, when you decide to start drawing from a pension, it can dramatically affect your success in overcoming inflation.

In general, a pension plan is an employee benefit in which the employer commits to making regular contributions to a pool of money that is set aside to fund payments made to eligible employees after they retire.[53] In these types of plans, the investment risk rests solely with the employer. It is up to the employer to appropriately contribute to the pension fund each year, and it is up to the pension fund manager to ensure that the funds bear enough interest to finance future payments.

There are two main types of pension plans: the defined-benefit plan and the cash-balance plan. The Department of Labor, Employee Benefits Security Administration, provides the following definitions of each plan.

- Defined-benefit plan: Such a plan is funded by the employer and promises to pay a specific monthly benefit at retirement that is normally calculated by using a formula that includes factors such as your salary, your age, and the number of years you worked at the company. For example, your pension benefit might be equal to your total years of service times 1 percent of your average salary for the final five years of employment.[54]
- Cash-balance plan: Also funded by the employer, this consists of "pay credits" (such as 5 percent of salary) and an "interest credit" (either a fixed rate or a variable rate that is linked to an index such as the one-year Treasury bill [T-bill] rate). Increases and decreases in the value of the plan's investments do not directly affect the benefit amounts promised to participants.[55]

Whereas a cash-balance pension plan provides an employee with a lump-sum benefit upon retirement with an option to forgo the lump sum in exchange for a monthly benefit, a defined-benefit pension plan provides an employee with the promise of monthly payments in retirement for life. Some, but not all, defined-benefit pension plans allow for a lump-sum distribution option. A defined-benefit pension plan is the most common plan and is the plan most people think of when they think of a pension plan. Because of this, we are going to spend most of our time discussing the defined-benefit pension plan.

Pension Funding And Protection

Let's go back to our three-legged stool in chapter 4 for a moment. If you recall, we had the three-legged stool that was. This was the ideal retirement for most of the twentieth century. Each leg of the stool, Social Security, a pension, and personal savings, provided balanced support for retirement. Here in the twenty-first century, our three-legged stool looks a bit different. We already covered the Social Security leg and why it's purchasing power has shrunk significantly. Social Security is underfunded and has a proven track record of not keeping up with inflation. Therefore, it will provide less and less income support as you go through retirement.

The pension leg has not only shrunk as well but is also illustrated by a dotted line. The dotted line, as stated in chapter 4, represents the fact that employer-provided pension plans have rapidly gone away since the 1980s. The shrinking of the pension leg represents challenges similar to those we highlighted with Social Security, but those challenges can be much more pronounced in the pension world.

Many pension plans have no built-in COLAs. Even though the COLAs provided by Social Security haven't kept up with inflation, it's still nice to know that some attempts have been made to combat inflation. No COLA means that the amount of the first check you receive from your pension is the same amount you will receive every month after. That is certainly not going to keep up with inflation. There are pensions that have COLAs, but in most cases, those COLAs aren't enough to keep up with inflation, so you still lose ground over time. Beyond that, many COLA programs are being cut to preserve pension funds, and that brings us to the most crucial point when it comes to pensions.

There is pervasive underfunding when it comes to pension plans across the United States. Simply put, many pension plans do not have the necessary assets to back up their current liabilities. Underfunded pension plans do not have enough money to pay out the promises made to those who retire under the plan.

As an example, the Civil Service Retirement System and the Federal Employees Retirement System, the two main federal government pension programs remain underfunded by billions if not trillions of dollars as of reported, compiled, and published November 2024. State and local government pension plans across the United States have $1.34 trillion in unfunded liabilities as of June 2024, and underfunded liabilities have been persistently over $1 trillion since 2008. Essentially, state and local pension funds have not been able to rebound since the Financial Crisis of 2008, despite a significant bull market run. Increasing contributions to the plans have not been enough to outpace the interest accruing on all the unfunded liabilities. Alternatively, private pension plans have rebounded in recent years, but many still remain underfunded. Part of the reason for the success in the private sector is that many companies have frozen their pension plans and are no longer continuing to take on new liabilities.

This is bad news for taxpayers and pension recipients alike. Here we have another example of how the horsemen ride together. For government pensions, the solution seems simple. Raise taxes. Raise taxes to fund the unfunded liabilities. You've heard the saying, "Robbing Peter to pay Paul." Raising taxes to fund those unfunded liabilities is a lot like that. Taxes could be raised on all taxpayers to cover the liabilities of the underfunded government pensions. This includes state and local pensions as well. By raising taxes on all taxpayers, those taxpayers who are not part of a government pension are subsidizing those who are.

Raising taxes can help ensure public pension recipients still receive their pensions. They will just get to keep less of it because their taxes have gone up. In the case of federal government pensions, another option is to print money to cover the underfunded liabilities. In this case, the horseman of inflation appears again, as we have already discussed, printing money can result in devaluing the purchasing power of the pension checks received. Don't forget about bracket creep either, which we discussed at the beginning of part 2 and will discuss further when we get to part 3 regarding the horseman of taxes. The horseman of taxes will be waiting to collect when the horseman of inflation pushes you to a higher tax bracket.

It is a bit of a different story for private pension recipients, which is why you need to pay special attention to your pension plan's annual funding notice. Each year, if you are part of a private-sector pension fund, the pension plan administrator is required to send out an annual funding notice to plan participants and beneficiaries. This notice provides information on how well the pension plan is funded, the value of the pension plan's assets and liabilities, how the pension assets are invested, and the legal limits on how much the Pension Benefit Guarantee Corporation (PBGC) can pay if the pension plan ends or becomes insolvent.[56]

The PBGC was created by the Employee Retirement Income Security Act of 1974 and acts as a financial safety net for private-sector pension plans. It is the backup to private-sector pension plans that go belly up. The PBGC only guarantees monthly benefits up to a certain limit, which depends on which type of pension plan you are under. The two types are single-employer pension plans and multiemployer pension plans. If you worked for a private company and weren't part of a union that provided the pension plan, you most likely fall under the single-employer pension plan category. If you were part of a union that included other workers in a similar craft (e.g., bricklayers, ironworkers, electricians, plumbers, transportation) but worked for different companies, you most likely fall under the multiemployer plan. This distinction is important because the two PBGC programs are funded and maintained separately.[57]

Single-Employer Program

Under the single-employer program, the PBGC collects insurance premiums from the company sponsoring the pension plan. This is to provide the PBGC with the resources necessary to back up the plans it is forced to take over and pay the benefits for.[58]

Many underfunded plans terminate because the employer has gone out of business, liquidated, or sold its assets in an insolvency situation. In other instances, lenders or other investors who are funding a bankruptcy workout will not participate in the reorganization unless the plan is terminated.[59]

Under the single-employer plan, the PBGC most likely isn't going to step in unless the company sponsoring the pension goes into bankruptcy. The PBGC doesn't want to take over a plan unless it absolutely must. As of 2024, the single-employer program had enough assets to cover the liabilities it had taken on. This is good news. What's important to pay attention to is how many plans the PBGC is forced to take over in the coming years. In 2021 alone, the PBGC assumed the responsibility for benefit payments of nearly thirty-four thousand workers and retirees in forty-seven single-employer plans.[60]

A notable single-employer plan taken over by the PBGC in recent history was Sears Holdings Corporation. On February 11, 2019, the PBGC took responsibility for the Sears Holding Corporation's two defined-benefit pension plans that cover workers and retirees of Sears, Roebuck and Co. and Kmart Corporation. The two plans cover about ninety thousand pension plan participants.[61] Before Sears filed for bankruptcy in 2018, the same year, Sears CEO Eddie Lampert cited the pension plan as one of the causes for the demise of the company. Since 2005, Sears has paid $4.5 billion to keep the pension plans going. Lampert argued that without the pension fund payments, "we would have been in a better position to compete with other large retail companies, many of which don't have large pension plans."[62] This is an important note. It isn't a stretch to think that other companies will look at Sears Holding Corporation as an example of what could happen to them if they don't get their pension liabilities under control. That often means cutting benefits to participants, which we see in the example below with General Electric (GE).

GE is another company that made headlines a few years ago because of its pension plan. In 2016, GE had the largest pension deficit among all S&P 500 companies, at $31 billion, which was $11 billion worse than the next closest company. Since then, GE has taken many steps to overcome this challenge. They froze pensions for current participants and moved to a defined-contribution plan such as a 401(k).

Freezing a pension plan is what a company does when it wants to cut expenses and reduce its liabilities under the pension plan. Companies also do this in order to discontinue offering a pension benefit to its employees. The two types of freezes a company will generally implement are a soft freeze or a hard freeze.

A soft freeze is when a company no longer allows new employees to participate in the pension plan but allows currently covered employees to continue. Under this type of freeze, currently covered employees will still see the value of their future monthly payments increase before they retire and start drawing on the pension.

A hard freeze means that, in addition to no longer allowing new employees to participate in the pension plan, currently covered employees no longer accrue benefits under the plan. A hard freeze means the pension is completely frozen. For participants currently under the plan, the value of their monthly benefit will no longer increase. The monthly benefit they will receive upon retirement is based on the benefit they have accrued up to the time the pension was frozen. No more increases are provided based on increased wages or years of service.

GE froze its plan to new entrants in 2012. This was a soft freeze. In 2019, the same year the PBGC took responsibility for the Sears Holdings Corporation's two defined-benefit pension plans that CEO Lambert attributed, at least in part, to the demise of the company, GE switched to a hard freeze and froze benefit increases for twenty thousand covered employees. GE also offered lump-sum buyouts to one hundred thousand retirees who had not yet started receiving their benefits in order to reduce the company's pension liability even further. This strategy alone helped GE reduce its pension deficit by $5 billion to $8 billion.[63]

Before a company issues a freeze, they must give participants notice at least forty-five days in advance. This is why it is important to pay attention to the correspondence you receive from your pension plan. You don't want something happening inside of your plan that you aren't aware of. Too many people make the mistake of setting things off to the side when they receive financial information they don't fully understand. They are busy with their jobs, families, and living life. They plan to get to it later but simply don't. That is why I tell all the families I serve that if you get something in the mail that you don't understand, send it to me. I'm happy to take a look, explain it, and help come up with a plan to act if one is necessary.

In the case of GE, they offered a lump-sum buyout when they froze the pension. Often, there is a time limit for participants to take advantage of this option. I've seen it far too many times where a family could have greatly benefited from the lump-sum option but waited too long to act. By the time they came to see me for planning, the window was closed, so please pay attention to letters you receive about your pension plan.

Under the single-employer program, if your pension is ever taken over by the PBGC, there is a cap on how large a monthly benefit the PBGC will pay. A participant's cap depends on factors such as age when the company entered bankruptcy, when the pension plan terminates and is handed over to the PBGC, and the elected benefit such as single-life or with a survivor option or other individual factors. It doesn't matter if a participant's expected benefit is higher than the maximum amount allowed by the PBGC. If the plan is under the care of the PGBC, the participant can only receive the maximum amount.

For participants over the maximum amount, they will see a reduction in their monthly benefit. The pension plan's annual statement includes the legal limits on how much the PBGC can pay if a pension plan ends or becomes insolvent. It's hard to overstate how important it is to pay attention to your pension plan annual statement and to review it with your financial advisor. You want to stay up to date on how well-funded your pension is and what kind of effects there might be if your pension plan is ever assumed by the PBGC.

Having an underfunded pension is a liability for companies in a multitude of ways. Besides knowing they will need to dump more money into the pension to fund the shortfall, the PBGC charges companies a higher premium if the pension is underfunded. Those premium requirements grow based on how underfunded the pension is. It doesn't take long for companies to feel like they won't be able to dig themselves out of the hole.

In planning, we often run scenarios that include what, if any, changes can be expected with the overall success of your retirement plan if your pension were to be taken over by the PBGC. This type of planning is important because life invariably throws curveballs. The more of them you anticipate, the better chance you have of knocking them out of the park.

Multiemployer Program

As stated, the multiemployer pension program operates differently and is managed separately from the single-employer program. As one might assume, a multiemployer pension is backed by several companies, not a single company like a single-employer pension. A multiemployer pension plan is created through an agreement among several employers and a union. Often, the companies that form these plans are in similar or related industries like transportation, manufacturing, or entertainment. Under the plan agreement, employers make contributions to the pension plan on behalf of the employees. The pension plan makes premium payments to the PBGC based on the number of participants covered by the plan as a way to protect participants in the event the pension plan becomes insolvent, in which case the PBGC could step in and ensure participants receive funds up to the guaranteed limit.[64]

On the surface, you might think that participants of multiemployer pension plans provide a higher level of protection to plan participants than single-employer plans. Conventional wisdom would dictate strength in numbers, but that isn't necessarily the case. In fact, the opposite has proven to be true.[65] In multiemployer plans, if one company withdraws from the pension or goes bankrupt, it can create a ripple effect through the entire pension fund. Companies inside multiemployer plans share the funding responsibility. If a company drops out of the plan, the share of funding responsibility increases for the remaining companies, thus increasing the liability for each company. This is known as "orphan liabilities,"[66] and it creates additional economic pressure for the companies that remain in the plan.

When a pension fund enters "critical" status, meaning it is funded less than sixty-five percent and is projected to have a funding deficiency within five years or an inability to pay benefits within seven years,[67,68] a surcharge of 5 to 10 percent is imposed on employer contributions.[69] This makes funding the plan even more expensive for employers. Based on these factors alone, it is easy to see why the PBGC reports that the average multiemployer plan is far less well-funded than the average single-employer plan.

Additional factors have also contributed to the underfunding of multiemployer pension funds. Industries have seen a shift to nonunion workers. This means less money is being contributed to the pension plan on behalf of young employees. Other industries and companies have had a decline in workforce due to broad industry declines or automation. Again, that means less funds being contributed to the pension fund. To try and make up for lower contribution amounts, some funds have switched to investing in diversified portfolios, which include investments outside of the traditional government securities or other "risk-free" investments. This change dramatically increased the investment risk inside of the funds.

While this change makes sense in theory, allowing plans to take greater advantage of positive years in the market, it also makes the funds more susceptible to losses. Therefore, the Great Recession of 2007–2009 really hurt pension fund assets as a whole, increasing the funding deficit.[70] Improved market performance can help bolster pension funds. In 2024, for example, pensions recorded an average annual return of 10.3 percent, exceeding expectations. Nonetheless, the public pension system still faced a shortfall exceeding $1 trillion.[71]

Just like government-backed pensions, multiemployer pensions seem to have a trump card that private or single-employer pension plans do not, and that is the government itself. Before the passing of the American Rescue Plan Act of 2021, the PBGC's multiemployer insurance program was projected to be insolvent by 2026. With an estimated $74 to $91 billion of assistance provided to eligible multiemployer plans by the American Rescue Plan (ARP), the system will be propped up for several more decades, with solvency estimates running for forty years.

This is good news if you are part of a multiemployer pension plan, but those billions of dollars come from somewhere. Quite likely, that infusion of cash into the system could lead to greater inflation and higher taxes.

PBGC Maximum Amount

My grandfather, Harry Ford, was born and raised in Steubenville, Ohio, and worked for Weirton Steel as a manual laborer for over forty years. As a participant of the pension plan, when he retired, he started receiving a monthly check that was supposed to be guaranteed for life. Unfortunately, on Monday, May 19, 2003, Weirton Steel filed for Chapter 11 bankruptcy, and the Weirton Steel Corporation retirement plan was taken over by the PBGC.

Whether you are part of a single-employer plan like Weirton Steel or a multiemployer plan, if your pension is taken over by the PBGC due to a lack of funding, you could receive a reduction in benefits. Congress sets the maximum guarantee amount each year for single-employer plans[72,73] and a formula is used for multiemployer plans, which can be found on the PBGC website.[74]

When my grandfather's pension was taken over, the maximum monthly benefit for a sixty-five-year-old was $3,664.77. My grandfather had worked for Weirton Steel from the time he was sixteen years old, after dropping out of high school, so he could provide financial support for his family. None of that mattered. The only thing that mattered was the fact that his monthly pension exceeded the maximum amount allowed by Congress for a single-employer plan now under PBGC control, and his benefit was reduced.

Based on the examples provided on the PBGC's website, it isn't out of the question for someone in a multiemployer plan to see their annual benefit reduced by 30 to 40 percent![75] That's a big hit. It can be made worse if you never expected or planned for it.

This is why it is so important to review the annual report sent out by your pension plan each year. The annual statement you receive on your pension will include details about the plan, its calculations, and how well-funded it is. You don't want to get caught off guard by an underfunded pension.

If one company goes bankrupt, it can create a ripple effect throughout the entire pension fund. Also, the passing of the

ARP may incentivize more companies to exit the pension fund. As described above, when a multiemployer pension fund enters "critical" status, a surcharge of 5 to 10 percent can be imposed on contributions.

When To Start Withdrawing From Your Pension

Just like Social Security, when you choose to start taking your pension is a personal decision, but there are a host of factors to consider before making that decision.

If you have read the chapters on Social Security, just know that many of the same factors apply. When and how you choose to take your pension can have a significant impact on how much you will receive from your pension over your lifetime, how well protected your spouse is if you happen to predecease him or her, how much in tax you will pay, how your retirement assets are affected, and ultimately, your probability of success in retirement.

Similar to Social Security's full retirement age, most pensions have a normal retirement date. Your normal retirement date is when you are eligible to receive the total benefit you have accrued under the plan. Some pension plans allow participants to start their benefits before their normal retirement date, but as you may have guessed, the effects of starting your pension early will likely mean a lower monthly payment. The impact of starting early depends on the plan. Reach out to your pension plan provider or human resources department to get the specifics of your plan. Some pension plans have online calculators you can use to run different scenarios.

Taking your benefit early at a reduced amount can put you behind in your battle against inflation for all the same reasons we discussed with Social Security. You'll receive a reduced amount for starting early. That penalty is for life, so it won't keep up with inflation. Most pension plans don't offer any kind of COLA, and if you are fortunate enough to have a pension that provides a COLA, they are still unlikely to keep up with inflation. By starting early at a reduced rate, you also put yourself further behind inflation by reducing the dollar-for-dollar amount of those cost-of-living adjustments.

Most pension plans have a normal retirement date of sixty-five. There are some exceptions, but that is the norm. You may have plans to retire before the age of sixty-five. That's great. As with Social Security, just because you retire before your pension's normal retirement date doesn't mean you have to start your pension as soon as you retire. It is important to integrate your pension into your overall financial plan. Instead of taking a reduction on your pension by taking it early, it may make sense to draw the funds you need exclusively from your retirement assets first, before starting your pension at the full amount later. Getting the full amount from your pension could reduce the amount you will need to take from your assets long-term, which can mean more funds available to you in the future. We saw this play out in our example with Steve and Linda in chapter 6 with Social Security.

How To Take Your Pension

How you take your pension is going to depend on factors such as how long your life expectancy is, if you are married, what other assets you have, and a few others.

As we noted earlier, nearly half of all pre-retirees underestimate their life expectancy by five years or more, so unless you have an extenuating circumstance, I typically recommend planning for a long life.[76] Longevity plays a role in when you take your pension because the longer you live, the more likely you want to ensure that you are getting the maximum monthly amount possible from your pension, especially given that most pensions aren't going to keep up with inflation. The day you start your pension is the day the horseman of inflation starts attacking your purchasing power, and the purchasing power of your pension will continue to erode over the course of your retirement.

There are typically up to three ways you can receive money from your pension plan, depending on what type of plan it is. You can elect an annuity option, which will provide you with monthly payments depending on the type of annuity option you elect. You may be eligible to elect to receive a lump-sum payment; instead of receiving monthly payments, you can elect to receive all the money up front. Lastly, some plans allow for a combination of the two previous options.

Annuity Options

When it comes to the annuity option, there are several sub-options to choose from. Typically, a plan is going to provide a single-life annuity option, survivorship options, or period-certain options. The single-life option generally provides the highest monthly payout and is guaranteed for the duration of the life of the retiree and no one else. With the single-life option, as soon as you pass, there is nothing else that continues, so if you are married, your spouse does not receive annuity payments. That can be bad news financially if a spouse depends on the income. With the single-life option, if you pass away sooner than expected and receive only a few payments, the benefit you spent years working to build up vanishes.

With a survivorship option, the benefit continues after you pass. Commonly, a spouse is the recipient of the survivorship option. With a survivorship annuity option, your monthly benefit is likely to be less than the single-life option, because now the pension plan is insuring payments for more than one life. Common survivorship options include 25 percent, 50 percent, 75 percent, and 100 percent survivor benefits.

Here's how it works: Let's assume your single-life option was $2,000 a month, but you want to ensure your spouse still gets something if you were to pass away. If you choose the 50 percent survivor annuity option, there will be a reduction in the monthly amount that you receive because there is more than one life that is being insured. Let's assume your benefit amount is $1,840 a month. If you pass, your spouse will receive $920 a month (50 percent of $1,840) for the rest of their life. The higher the percentage that continues to the survivor, the higher the discount on the original monthly payment.

Lastly, there are period certain annuity options. The option makes sure that whatever annuity payment you select will last for a certain number of years. For example, you might elect the 50 percent survivor annuity option with a twenty-year period certain. Even if you and your spouse pass before twenty years, the payments will continue on for a beneficiary until the twenty-year mark. Just like with the survivor options, a discount to your monthly amount will be assessed to account for the period certain guarantee.

If you are entitled to a pension, making the right decision on how and when to take it is an important one. It can be just as important a decision as when and how you start your Social Security benefit.

In my practice, I have come to an uncomfortable fact that I want to address here. Too often, I have seen husbands choose the single-life annuity option. That large monthly benefit without any discount is enticing. As men, we tend to think we are bulletproof. I'm reminded of a saying, "Women grow up. Men grow old." Even though the maximum monthly benefit is attractive, I have found it is not necessarily the best option for a retirement plan if you are planning for both spouses to have adequate income for the rest of their lives. I think that should be the goal of any plan. Sometimes, the single-life option does make the most sense because of other planning strategies that can be implemented, but it needs to be a part of a plan with a strategy regarding where the income will come from if a spouse passes prematurely.

Unfortunately, we don't always get to meet with families before they make certain decisions, and we need to make the best of a not-so-great situation.

I remember meeting Rick and Kathy for the first time. Rick was receiving a $30,000 annual pension. It was taken using the single-life option. The first question I asked was what their plan was to make up that income if, God forbid, Rick predeceased Kathy prematurely. They didn't have an answer. They hadn't given it much thought. Rick was not a bad guy. He cared deeply for his wife. They were both enticed by the large monthly income when it came time to make the pension election and figured everything would work out.

Rick passed at the age of seventy-two from a heart attack. Kathy is still here over six years later. Not only did she lose $30,000 a year, she also saw a reduction in Social Security income of $16,000. If you are keeping track, that's a $46,000 loss of income. It dramatically affected Kathy's standard of living and still does to this day.

I will mention this several times throughout these chapters. I want both spouses to successfully mitigate the horsemen, so please keep in mind the beginning of a legacy for most people starts with the spouse they leave behind. We want everyone's legacy to get off to a good start by making sure the surviving spouse is well taken care of.

Lump-Sum Option

Not all plans allow for a lump-sum option, but if your plan does, it is certainly worth running the numbers to determine if this is the right option for you. Instead of electing an annuity option to provide you with monthly income, the lump-sum option allows you to receive all your benefits up front, as discussed previously. Now, the first question you might be asking is, "If I receive all my benefits at once, won't I owe a massive amount in taxes?" The answer is no if you structure the lump-sum withdrawal correctly. If you elect the lump-sum option, you should be allowed to roll those funds into an individual retirement account (IRA) in your name. An IRA is a tax-advantaged savings account that helps you save for retirement. Typically, the money you put into the IRA is not taxed. It grows tax-deferred, and the tax is owed when you take withdrawals in retirement. By moving the lump sum into an IRA, it keeps the funds tax-deferred, meaning you only owe taxes when you withdraw the funds from that account.

The benefit of doing a lump-sum rollover is that the IRA is in your control. Investing involves risk, including the potential loss of principal, but leaving your funds in the pension plan isn't without its own risks. By moving the money into an IRA, you get to choose how the funds are invested instead of your assets being lumped together in the pension fund investment pool. It allows you to have a portfolio that is more tailor-made to your needs. You can also control the flow of income. Maybe you don't need $2,000 a month as in our previous example. Maybe you don't need monthly income at all, but want to be able to tap into your funds for non-periodic expenses like home repairs, Christmas, or travel.

A lump-sum rollover also takes away the risk that the pension plan may one day be taken over by the PBGC. You won't have to worry about a benefit reduction because you already received your benefit upfront.

A drawback of doing the lump-sum rollover is that if you are after the maximum monthly benefit amount guaranteed for life, the lump-sum option isn't going to provide that. In our previous example, we were looking at a single-life benefit of $2,000 a month. Let's say the lump-sum option was $300,000. A 5 percent withdrawal on $300,000 is only $15,000 a year or $1,250 a month.

Again, determining whether or not taking the lump-sum option is right for you comes down to running your numbers. If you can produce enough income from Social Security, your other investments, and the lump-sum option to maintain your standard of living, most of the time, taking the lump-sum option is going to be the recommendation for the reasons listed previously. An income stream can be created from the lump sum that is in your control. It eliminates the risk of the pension being taken over by the PBGC, and it puts you more in control of your tax situation. You will only be taxed when you take a withdrawal.

For some families, the lump-sum option is out of the question because they simply don't have the ability to make up the income they need outside of taking the monthly benefit. Just like with Social Security, we run multiple scenarios, comparing taking a monthly distribution versus taking the lump-sum option. We use the planning process to travel to the future to see which option is likely to be the better option for you.

Making Your Pension Work For You

Fewer and fewer retirees are entitled to a pension each year, but if you are eligible for a pension in retirement, it is important to get it right. When and how you take your pension can mean the difference between a successful retirement plan and an unsuccessful retirement plan, and no one wants to face the prospect of running out of money before they run out of life. Run your numbers, run your numbers, run your numbers.

In the battle against the horsemen, running your numbers is crucial. Just remember, bad inputs make bad data. Garbage in, garbage out, so when you run your numbers, ensure the inputs are accurate.

Chapter Eight

PERSONAL SAVINGS

I n previous chapters, I used the image of the three-legged stool, a retirement plan that included the legs of Social Security, pension, and personal savings as the three most common sources of income supporting retirement. Throughout much of the twentieth century, these legs were relatively balanced, but that is no longer the case. Currently, for most Americans, the situation is much less the image of a three-legged stool and more an image of the pillar of personal savings as the main resource for a retirement plan. If the horsemen are going to be kept at bay, it is likely going to depend heavily on your personal savings.

The pillar of personal savings is the culmination of every financial decision—good and bad—you have made over the course of your life. Don't be alarmed. No one makes perfect decisions 100 percent of the time. Thankfully, you don't have to have made all the right decisions to have a successful retirement. Life happens. Sometimes, decisions must be made out of necessity and survival, even though they may not be the most beneficial in the long run. Hopefully, on balance, you are making good decisions. Hopefully, these next chapters on personal savings will be of help in your decision-making about retirement.

Here are some of the big decisions you make over the course of your lifetime. Is the house paid off or on its way to being paid off prior to or shortly after retirement? Are you carrying credit card debt, or is the credit card paid off each month? Have you spent most of your life living above your means, or have you taken a little bit from each paycheck and put it aside to accumulate a nest egg? Have you taken loans against your retirement? Are you carrying any personal, student, or automobile loans?

Personal savings is all about the decisions, big and small, that build your assets. What are the common assets that make up the personal savings pillar?

Sources Of Personal Savings

Perhaps the most common asset of all is an employer-sponsored, defined-contribution plan known as the 401(k). On November 6, 1978, Congress passed the Revenue Act, which paved the way for what we now know as a 401(k) plan. This allowed companies to shift the responsibility of helping families save for retirement through the traditional defined-benefit pension plan onto the shoulders of the employees themselves by allowing them to contribute to an employer-sponsored plan known as a 401(k) plan. By 1983, only five years after the Revenue Act was passed, nearly half of all large firms offered or considered offering a 401(k) plan because it was a cheaper and more efficient option for them compared to all the requirements, maintenance, cost, and unpredictability of running a pension plan.[77]

By 1996, 401(k) plan assets passed the $1 trillion mark, and today, there is over $4.8 trillion saved in 401(k) plans across the country.[78]

A 401(k) isn't the only kind of defined contribution plan. Your employer might offer a 403(b), SIMPLE IRA, Thrift Savings Plan, deferred compensation plan, profit sharing plan, stock bonus plan, employee stock ownership plan, or 457 plan. Each one has its differences, but for now, we'll lump them together, so even if you have one of the other plans besides a 401(k), don't worry; the employer-sponsored contribution plan that you do have still applies.

Other common retirement assets include traditional IRAs, Roth IRAs, and individual and joint brokerage accounts. We defined traditional IRAs in the pension section. A Roth IRA is another type of tax-advantaged savings account that helps you save for retirement. With a Roth IRA, the money is taxed when you put it in, but then it grows tax-free. As long as you follow the rules,[79] you'll be able to take withdrawals in retirement that are completely tax-free in the future. That means what you put in plus the growth.

Individual and joint brokerage accounts are not specifically designed to fund retirement like an IRA, but that doesn't mean you can't use the funds to help supplement your income in retirement. With a brokerage account, you have already paid the tax on the money you put it, and that becomes your principal or cost basis. If your money grows and you sell out an investment, you will likely have to pay some capital gains tax on that gain, even if you don't withdraw the money. Brokerage accounts are not tax-deferred.

You might also have some money saved at the bank in a money market account or certificates of deposit (CDs). This isn't an exhaustive list. Some companies offer unique plans for highly compensated employees, including employee stock purchase plans and stock options. It's important to know exactly what type of assets make up your retirement accounts because, as we will find out when we discuss the horseman of taxes, different types of accounts can have radically different tax implications.

Regardless of what type of accounts you have, the financial success of your retirement depends not only on how much you have saved but the successful management of what you have saved. Making sure income from personal savings lasts through your lifetime is a difficult task. We mustn't forget about the horseman of longevity. Remember, there is a 50 percent chance that one spouse in a married couple turning age sixty-five today will make it to age ninety-two, and as we will discuss during our section on the horseman of healthcare, there is ample evidence that the 50 percent probability is going to be increasing.

How Much For Retirement?

I'm often asked, "Spencer, how much do we need to have saved for retirement?" Wouldn't it be nice to know your exact number? With solid personal financial retirement planning, you can arrive at a number, but getting there takes some legwork. According to Fidelity, by age sixty-seven, you should have around ten times (10x) your preretirement income specifically set aside for retirement. If you make $100,000 a year, you should have at least $1,000,000 saved for retirement.

For benchmarking purposes, Fidelity's age-based milestones are as follows:

By age 30: 1x your income
By age 40: 3x your income
By age 50: 6x your income
By age 60: 8x your income[80]

Maybe the concept of having 10x of your preretirement income saved before retirement is good news for you because you have done a fantastic job of saving. For most families, that isn't the case. According to Empower, a large employer-sponsored plan service provider, the average sixty to sixty-five-year-old has $198,194 saved in their 401(k). If the benchmark is ten times preretirement income, that equates to the average sixty to sixty-five-year-old only making $19,819.40 a year.

That number doesn't bear up to scrutiny, which means a lot of families are behind in their quest to save an adequate amount for retirement. If you fall into the former category and you are on pace to have ten times your preretirement income or more saved, that would be fantastic. There is a clear path to a successful retirement plan for you. If you are in the latter category and are trying to catch up, you aren't necessarily doomed to work the rest of your life. The good news is that there are ways to help create income streams to make up for shortfalls in personal savings, but there are limitations.

The Two Halves Of Your Financial Life

When it comes to the pillar of personal savings, it represents so much of what you have done to prepare for a successful retirement. You go through two distinct phases in your financial life. In our practice, we articulate it by saying that there are two halves. First is the accumulation phase. You're typically in this phase between ages eighteen to fifty-five. In this phase, you are younger. You're working. You have a paycheck coming in. If the market takes a tumble, you aren't happy about it, but you still have that paycheck coming in to back you up and time on your side to let your investments recover.

The second half of your financial life, typically between the age of fifty-five and the end of life, is the distribution phase. In this phase, you are closer to retirement or you are in retirement. You are nearing the time or may already be at the point where you no longer have a paycheck coming in, but your investments are your paycheck. You're no longer putting money in; you're taking money out. That one-hundred-and-eighty-degree shift also requires that same shift in your investment strategy.

There was an article published on MarketWatch titled, "Is Your Advisor Still Right for Your Retirement?" with the subtitle, "The financial pro who gets you to your golden years may not be the right one to get you through them. Here's how to tell."[81] It's a well-researched article, and if you would like to read it in its entirety, you can find it at thefourhorsemenbook. com. The article highlights the importance of making sure you are working with someone who knows and understands how to manage a portfolio in the second half of your financial life.

The recipe for the first half is relatively simple for an advisor: help families put away a little bit of money over a long period of time so it can grow into a nest egg. Now, just because the recipe is simple doesn't mean the job is easy. However, that being said, as one of the interviewees of the article points out, "the distribution phase of retirement—the time when you withdraw funds from savings—makes the accumulation part look like child's play."

There is more at stake during the distribution phase. The mandate for the accumulation phase is to grow the portfolio. The mandate for the distribution phase is to produce adequate income, reduce taxes, and protect the principal, all while growing the portfolio, and oh, by the way, you have to continue to fulfill all those mandates over a twenty-to-thirty-year period. That's a tall task, and in my opinion there are simply not enough advisors trained to help you accomplish that feat, which is why the article encourages families to ensure they choose an advisor who is up to the job.

Why Investing In The Second Half Is (Or Should Be) Different

I want to provide some examples to really highlight the difference between investing in the first half of your financial life compared to the second half because it's hard to overstate how damaging it can be to your financial goals and livelihood if you never make the adjustment from first-half investing to second-half investing when the time comes.

Let's say you are getting ready to retire, and you have $1,000,000 saved. Assume that based on what you are receiving from your other sources of income, you need to take a 4 percent withdrawal or $40,000 from your retirement accounts to maintain your standard of living. Nothing wrong with that, with a properly structured plan. However, suppose no one ever had a conversation with you about the difference between investing for the first half of your financial life and the second half of your financial life. You go into retirement invested as though you are in the first half of your financial life. In reality, you should be investing as though you are in the second half. If, the first year of your retirement, the market declines 20 percent, then so does your portfolio. Your $1,000,000 turns into $800,000.

If this were the first half, there would be no reason to panic. You're still receiving a paycheck and have time on your side to hopefully recover. In the second half, you still need to take that $40,000 to live on, so after the 20 percent decline and your $40,000 withdrawal, your total is $760,000. Next year, you still need the $40,000, plus the horseman of inflation requires his premium. As we discussed previously, the Federal Reserve's goal is to keep inflation around 2 percent. That's the goal. It is not a guarantee that we can rely on, so, for example, we'll assume inflation of 3 percent. That means you need another $1,200.

After an initial drop of 20 percent, an initial distribution rate of 4 percent or $40,000 a year, plus 3 percent inflation, if you were going to be back to your $1,000,000 at the end of five years, it would take a cumulative return of just under 49 percent. That's an average return of a little over 12 percent a year—a tall task to say the least. Chances are, it would take you a lot longer than five years to fully recover, if you ever recovered at all. Keep in mind that on your path to recovery, you'll probably run into some more years when the market is down, extending your time to break even. That is the risk of staying invested like you're in the first half of your financial life as opposed to being invested for the second half.

For comparison, let's look at someone who is in the first half of their financial life with the same $1,000,000 portfolio. They experience the same 20 percent decline, but they don't have to take income. The $1,000,000 they've saved turns into $800,000. They aren't happy, but their paycheck is all they need. In order for their account to be fully recovered at the end of the five-year period, they would need a cumulative return of just under 23 percent or an average of less than 6 percent a year. They would need less than half the growth to recover than if they were taking income, making it far easier for them to break even and see continued growth.

First Half Versus Second Half Financial Life Outcomes

Year	Still Working, Not Taking Income		Retired And Taking Income		
	Market Return	Investment Balance	Market Return	Investment Balance	Income
0		$1,000,000		$1,000,000	
1	-20%	$800,000	-20%	$760,000	$40,000
2	5.74%	$845,898	12.23%	$811,756	$41,200
3	5.74%	$894,428	12.23%	$868,605	$42,436
4	5.74%	$945,744	12.23%	$931,135	$43,709
5	5.74%	$1,000,003	12.23%	$1,000,002	$45,020
Cumulative Return Year 2-5	22.95%		48.92%		

Note: 5.74% is rounded up from 5.7372%. 12.23% is rounded down from 12.231%.

(Hypothetical examples shown for illustrative purposes only and don't reflect any specific product or investment, nor do they account for investment fees or taxes)

Sequence Risk

Sequence risk is not knowing when the good versus the bad years in the market are going to come. When taking income, you are much more susceptible to the downside of sequence risk, which is alluded to in the previous example. What happens if you are unfortunate to retire when the market is in a period of decline instead of retiring when the market is on its way up?

Take this sequence of returns for example:

- Year 1: -22 percent
- Year 2: -9 percent
- Year 3: +8 percent
- Year 4: +11 percent
- Year 5: +7 percent
- Year 6: +20 percent
- Year 7: +15 percent
- Year 8: -9 percent
- Year 9: +17 percent
- Year 10: +22 percent

We'll use some of the same numbers from our previous example. Suppose you had $1,000,000 saved for retirement, and you planned to take a 4 percent withdrawal or $40,000 a year. You also planned to increase that $40,000 by 3 percent a year to combat inflation. By the end of the third year, your $1,000,000 will be worth $640,340. If you were brave enough to continue the ride, by the end of year ten, you would have $883,203. You averaged a return of 6 percent per year. Your plan was to start off by only taking a 4 percent withdrawal plus a little extra for inflation each year, and you ended with $116,797 less than what you started with.

Now, what if we took those same exact returns and just put them in reverse order? In this scenario, the good years come first instead of the bad years. By the end of year ten, after taking all the same exact withdrawals and averaging 6 percent, you have $1,186,663. That's $186,663 more than what you started with and $303,460 more than with the previous order of market returns.

That is the significance of sequence risk. If the bad years come first, you have less money available to receive the positive benefits of compounding interest, which could force you into a downward cycle that may not be possible to recover from. Because we don't know when the bad years versus the good years are going to come, one of the best ways to address sequence risk is to smooth out the ride overall. That is what second-half investing is all about.

Sequence Risk						
Year	Market Returns	Investment Balance	Income	Market Returns In Reverse	Investment Balance	Income
0		$1,000,000			$1,000,000	
1	-22%	$740,000	$40,000	22%	$1,180,000	$40,000
2	-9%	$632,200	$41,200	17%	$1,339,400	$41,200
3	8%	$640,340	$42,436	-9%	$1,176,418	$42,436
4	11%	$667,068	$43,709	15%	$1,309,172	$43,709
5	7%	$668,743	$45,020	20%	$1,525,986	$45,020
6	20%	$756,121	$46,371	7%	$1,586,434	$46,371
7	15%	$821,777	$47,762	11%	$1,713,180	$47,762
8	-9%	$698,622	$49,195	8%	$1,801,039	$49,195
9	17%	$766,717	$50,671	-9%	$1,588,275	$50,671
10	22%	$883,203	$52,191	-22%	$1,186,663	$52,191
Average Return	6%			6%		

(Hypothetical examples shown for illustrative purposes only and don't reflect any specific product or investment, nor do they account for investment fees or taxes)

When you are taking withdrawals, the downside tends to hurt you a little worse than the upside helps you. You may start to think, "Spencer, you are just showing an extreme example. That's not how it works in real life." However, keep in mind that if you retired at the beginning of 2000, you started with three years of substantial losses. Beginning in 2000, the S&P 500 posted three back-to-back years of negative returns: -9.10 percent in 2000, -11.89 percent in 2001, and -22.10 percent in 2002.[82] That's a cumulative loss of 43.09 percent. And what if you retired at the worst possible time, in October of 2007? The first thing you experienced was a seventeen-month-long decline resulting in a loss of 56.8 percent.[83] How about more recently? If you retired at the beginning of 2022, the S&P 500 dropped -18.11 percent,[84] with the NASDAQ dropping 32.97 percent.[85] Based on the history of the markets, the examples above are relatively tame.

In fact, if you were unfortunate enough to retire at the beginning of 2000 with $1,000,000 saved for retirement and planned to take out $40,000 a year plus an additional 2 percent each year for inflation, by the end of 2023, your $1,000,000 would be worth $628,688 based on the returns of the S&P 500 over that timeframe. Your lowest point over that twenty-four-year period was $389,814. That was at the end of 2008, and a lot of families weren't brave enough to continue to let their assets ride. They pulled their money, locking in that large loss without the chance of any recovery, and that is only taking 2 percent a year for inflation. The story looks a lot worse if you need more than that for inflation.

Another fun fact, just to again highlight the effects of sequence risk. If you reversed the returns over that twenty-four-year period that I just described. Using the same $1,000,000 initial savings balance and the same income, $40,000 plus 2 percent for inflation. Using the same returns, just reversed. At the end of the period, you would have $3,152,104!

To watch me walk through this example and others in more detail, please visit thefourhorsemenbook.com.

Smoothing Out The Second-Half Ride

As stated above, one of the best ways to help address sequence risk is to attempt to smooth out the ride, specifically to mitigate the losses. In times of decline in the market, you may have heard someone say, rather annoyingly, I might add, that you haven't really lost money unless you sell or realize the loss. The loss is just on paper. Well, that's all well and good in the first half of your financial life, but in the second half, when you are taking income, you are realizing those losses, at least to some extent.

In the first half of your financial life, if you own one hundred shares of ABC company and those shares decline by 20 percent, you can hold onto those one hundred shares until they recover their value. In the second half, assume you own one hundred shares of ABC company, and those shares decline by 20 percent, and you must take income. Well, after selling some shares to produce that income, you may only have ninety-five shares left. That's five fewer shares that get to participate in the potential recovery. That is going to dramatically extend the time horizon for you to break even, if you ever do, and that is why the losses hurt so much. Maintaining a decent rate of return while mitigating losses is necessary if you are going to mitigate both the horseman of longevity and inflation.

So, what can we do? Our goal is to smooth out the ride, but before we get to that, we need to talk about the three attributes of money.

The Three Attributes Of Money

There are three attributes when it comes to saving or investing money. The first attribute is easy to identify. Why do any of us invest our money, to begin with? Growth opportunity is the first attribute of investing money. The goal of investing is to see our money grow.

Yet, the further we run toward growth, the further we run from the second attribute, which is important, especially in retirement, and that is protection. Protection is the second attribute of investing your money. With investment comes risk, so you want to do what you can to balance the downside potential with upside potential. There are ways to bend this rule, which we will discuss, but it is a rule that rarely, if ever, can be broken.

The further we run toward protection, the further we generally run away from the third attribute of investing, which is liquidity. Do you have access to your money, or is it tied up where there is a penalty to withdraw that money?

There is no perfect investment vehicle that is going to neatly maximize all three attributes of investing your money—no silver bullet, no magic potion. Typically, the more you prioritize one specific attribute, the more likely the other two attributes are going to suffer. Based on my experience, as long as you don't prioritize one attribute too heavily, you can get a healthy dose of two of the three attributes in a single investment, but not all three.

If someone presents you with an awesome new product that is going to solve all your problems, run away. While no single investment covers growth, protection, and liquidity all at once, you can build a plan and a portfolio that includes a blend of all three attributes.

The Three Attributes Of Money

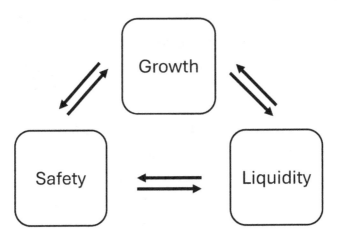

For example, if you are looking for growth potential and liquidity, you can invest in stocks. You can pull your money when you want to. It can grow over time, but it's not going to be safe from the downside and you can lose money. If you are looking for growth potential and protection, one potential vehicle for that might be real estate. Property values tend to increase over time. There are some downturns, but overall, real estate has shown to be less volatile than the market.[86] Plus, it provides income in the form of rent. It isn't always easily liquidated, though.

Maybe you are looking for protection and liquidity. A bank account accomplishes that goal, but you will be giving up some growth potential.

We are looking for balance, and balance is what helps to smooth out the ride. When you are investing for the first half, you can usually afford to neglect the attributes of protection and even liquidity. That's not how it works in the second half. When it comes to the three attributes of money, you need to ensure you are getting the right money in the right place at the right time. We've already talked about why protecting from the downside is so important, which is protection, and if you're going to be taking income, you should be concerned about liquidity, too. So, what might smoothing out the ride look like?

The Balancing Act Of The Second Half

In the second half of your financial life, no attribute should be neglected. If you are going to successfully mitigate the horsemen, you are going to need growth, protection, and liquidity. You'll need growth so you can provide yourself with raises to help keep up with inflation, and we haven't even touched yet on the horseman of taxes. You'll need protection so you can keep your income consistent in periods of market decline. A portfolio going backward without a safety net gives the advantage to the horseman of longevity. And, you need liquidity so you can live.

Let's take the same sequence of market returns we used in our previous example. Except, this time, instead of keeping 100 percent of the money in the market, we use protected, guaranteed vehicles for 50 percent of the money while keeping the other 50 percent directly invested for growth in the market.

Now the combined returns look like this:

- Year 1: -14.25 percent
- Year 2: -4.50 percent
- Year 3: +8 percent
- Year 4: +10.75 percent
- Year 5: +7 percent
- Year 6: +16 percent
- Year 7: +13.50 percent
- Year 8: -4.5 percent
- Year 9: +14.50 percent
- Year 10: +17 percent

(Hypothetical example shown for illustrative purposes only and does not reflect any specific product or investment, nor does it account for investment fees or taxes)

You still start with $1,000,000. You still need to take $40,000 a year plus an additional 3 percent compounded to fight off inflation, but instead of having $883,203 at the end of ten years like our first example, you have $1,049,074. That's after taking a total of $458,555 worth of withdrawals over that ten-year period.

As you can see, by having a portion of the money protected, you can help mitigate your downside risk. Instead of realizing 100 percent of the downside, you only captured 58 percent of the downside. Don't get me wrong, being down 14.25 percent or $142,500 on a million dollars in a single year isn't fun, but you can likely recover from that more easily than being down the full 22 percent. The tradeoff is you aren't going to capture as much of the potential upside. In our example, you only captured just under 87 percent of the upside of the market returns we previously used.

A further point is that in our first example, with all the money in the market, the average return was 6 percent per year. In the example of keeping a portion of the money protected, the average annual return is 6.35 percent. Protecting a portion of your money from the downside increased your average return overall. There is tremendous power in protecting yourself from the downside, and this is especially true when you're taking income.

At this time, a logical question you might be asking yourself is, "OK, so what's the protected money invested in?" Let's talk about some of those options.

The Protected Money

Most investors have a basic understanding of what growth money looks like mainly because the majority, if not all, of their investment life to this point has been in the first half, the accumulation phase, of their financial life. Growth money is typically made up of stocks, exchange-traded funds (ETFs), and mutual funds, among other investments. It's higher risk in the pursuit of higher reward.

If you want to learn more about growth money, please visitthefourhorsemenbook.com.

Protected money aims to provide a greater amount of principal protection without giving up too much of the upside. Protected money can be made up of several sources, which include cash, money market accounts, CDs, T-bills, Treasury bonds, corporate and municipal bonds, multi-year guaranteed annuities (MYGAs), market-linked CDs, buffered ETFs, and fixed indexed annuities (FIAs). There's more than just these that fit inside the category of protected money. In fact, we'll talk about an additional vehicle when we get to the horseman of healthcare, but for now, this list should suffice as some of the most common vehicles used for protection from losses.

Each option has its pros and cons. Cash is safe and liquid, but it isn't going to grow. In fact, the longer you sit on cash, the more purchasing power you lose due to the horseman of inflation. Money market accounts offer a little more growth than cash, but you probably won't be earning enough to overcome inflation. CDs offer even a little more growth than cash and money market accounts. Your principal is protected by the FDIC, but your purchasing power is not. Remember, inflation often operates in silence. It looks like you haven't lost any money. It may even look like you have made money, but if you aren't beating inflation, you are losing purchasing power. Your money is only worth what it can buy. If it buys less and less, it is worth less and less, even if your dollar amount is growing. You likely won't be earning enough interest in those bank CDs to keep up with inflation.

T-bills and Treasury bonds are considered some of most protected investments you can own because they are backed by the full faith and credit of the United States government. To some, that may sound laughable, but we are still the eight-hundred-pound gorilla in the room. We boast the world's largest economy, making up 26.3 percent of the 2024 global gross domestic product[87] while comprising only 4.23 percent of the world's population.[88] We have our problems. I'm not discounting that. We will cover more of that when we get to the horseman of taxes, but for now, there is no place else I'd rather be rich and no place else I'd rather be poor than the good old USA. We are still the land of opportunity. People fight their way to get into our country in the hopes of a better life for a reason. My father's college professor used to tell him, "When the United States economy gets a cold, the rest of the world gets pneumonia." It's still true, which is why I believe we can continue to be confident in US markets in the long term.

The good news about T-bills and Treasury bonds is that they provide principal protection. The bad news is, they typically don't offer enough upside to keep up with inflation. For example, over the past ten years, ten-year T-bill rates have averaged 2.32 percent.[89] Inflation has averaged 2.7 percent over that same timeframe.[90]

Bonds offer the opportunity to receive interest as well as grow in value, but bonds can also decline in value. Allow me to recall a performance factor from 2022. The US aggregate bond index was down 13.02 percent[91] at a time when the S&P 500 finished down 18.11 percent.[92] Still less risky than the market, a loss of 13.02 percent is notably not a loss of 18.11 percent, but bonds still captured 72 percent of the downside. To add insult to injury, while the S&P 500 has averaged a return of 13.14 percent over the past ten years, the US aggregate bond index only averaged 1.67 percent. The horseman of inflation could easily overtake that kind of average. This isn't meant to be the be-all and end-all discussion about bonds. You can buy individual bonds and hold them until maturity, but bonds aren't necessarily as safe an investment as many common investors think. There is still risk.

Before we move on to the rest of the list, I want to pause. All the protected money options we have discussed so far are not inherently bad investments. Having some cash on hand, some money in a checking account, savings account, and possibly some in bank CDs is necessary for a well-built financial plan. Everyone needs an emergency fund, and often, these accounts are the ones you can get money from the quickest. That's where liquidity or access comes into play.

T-bills, Treasury bonds, corporate bonds, and municipal bonds can still be appropriate investments for a segment of your protected money. If held to maturity, you get exactly what you signed up for: a principal-protected vehicle that provides interest. You just want to ensure you are getting the timing right.

In addition to that, during periods in which interest rates are on the decline, bonds tend to provide more capital appreciation as well as a fixed interest rate, so right now, we could be in a period where the timing is good for bond investments. Markets aren't static. They ebb and flow, so having a plan that can adapt is essential.

Additional Protected Money Options

Multi-year guaranteed annuities (MYGAs), market-linked CDs, buffered ETFs, and FIAs are also vehicles that are part of the protected bucket. I saved these for last because the average investor tends to be less familiar with these vehicles. These are often prime second-half financial life tools. You likely wouldn't have much use for them during the first half of your financial life when accumulation was the primary focus. Now that the focus is on accumulation, protection, and liquidity, these vehicles may fill a role in the protected money space. Still, they have their pros and cons. Remember, there is no perfect vehicle, but if you are someone who is open to learning new things and considering additional options, keep reading.

MYGAs

In my professional opinion, MYGAs are similar to CDs in that they offer principal protection and a fixed interest rate for a defined period of time. Instead of putting your money on deposit at a bank, you are purchasing a fixed, insurance-based product with an insurance company. Based on my professional experience, there are many differences between banks and insurance companies. One key difference is that banks accept short-term deposits and make long-term loans. Because of this, there is a mismatch between a bank's liabilities and assets. Insurance companies don't have this same problem, as they have a longer-term outlook. Therefore, much of the time, you can find a better fixed interest rate with an insurance company using a MYGA than you can at a bank using a CD.

A couple of other key benefits are that if you aren't taking a withdrawal, the tax on the interest of a MYGA is able to be deferred until you withdraw the funds. This can provide for some tax planning opportunities. If you need to withdraw, many MYGAs offer up to 10 percent liquidity each year, meaning you can take out 10 percent of the account value without penalty.[93,94] That means this portion of your money is a lot more accessible than your typical CD, where only the interest is able to be withdrawn during the term.

There are still restrictions and terms with MYGAs, as with every financial product. Even with a potentially higher interest rate, MYGAs may still struggle to keep up with inflation. The rates offered on MYGAs are still linked to the interest rate environment of the day. If we are in a low-interest rate environment, chances are the fixed interest rate offered on a

MYGA, is not going to be able to keep up with inflation in the long term.

MYGAs have surrender penalties, which are fees imposed when the annuity contract is canceled or when more than the allowable funds are withdrawn early. Common surrender penalties for a bank CD are anywhere from three to twelve months of interest. If you surrender a MYGA two years into a five-year term, your surrender penalty could be as high as 8 percent or greater of the total account value. This is mainly due to the fact that annuities are long-term retirement income vehicles, and insurance companies are more likely to invest for longer terms than banks, as we mentioned above. MYGAs may be a suitable option for a portion of your protected money, but it shouldn't make up the entirety of your protected-money strategy.

Market-Linked CDs

Purchasing insurance products is a new topic for many of those entering the second half of their financial lives. When you think of insurance, your mind probably goes to property and casualty insurance, things like home, auto, and life insurance. People often don't think about an insurance company as a place to save for retirement, but many of them provide competitive, protected money options. Another way to think about it is this. You insure your home, your car, and your life. Why wouldn't you also want some insurance for your retirement?

Market- or equity-linked CDs are investment vehicles that are purchased for a fixed sum of money and held for a set amount of time, similar to CDs you might purchase at the bank. Like with bank CDs, your principal is typically protected, but instead of receiving a fixed interest rate, your investment is linked to the returns of an underlying index like the S&P 500. There's no guarantee you will earn any interest.

Market-linked CDs have the power to provide greater upside potential than regular CDs, but there are some drawbacks. To name a few, they are illiquid during the term, meaning you aren't able to take income, and there are penalties if you cash out early. It's safe to say that most protected investments that offer protection of your principal are going to have some penalties if you need or decide to exit early.

Buffered ETFs

A third—and lesser-known—protected vehicle is the buffered ETF. This was first introduced by Innovator in 2018[95] and has since exploded in the marketplace, with more than $45 billion invested into the strategy.[96] There's a good reason for this. Buffered ETFs, also known as defined-outcome ETFs, take some of the unpredictability out of the market.

You may be familiar with regular ETFs that track an index like the S&P 500, Nasdaq, Dow Jones, Russell 2000, etc. Instead of buying each stock in the index, an ETF pools the investments, so you can buy one investment, the ETF, instead of buying each stock in the index. Another benefit is that buying a share of this pooled investment is much less expensive than trying to buy each individual stock that makes up the index. You get more diversification for fewer dollars. The downside is if you buy an ETF that tracks an index, you are taking on the full risk of that index. If you buy an ETF that tracks the S&P 500 index and the index grows 20 percent, your ETF investment will also likely grow 20 percent. However, if the index drops 20 percent, your ETF investment will likely also drop 20 percent. What if you want to participate in the performance of the index but not take on all the risk? This is where a buffered ETF comes in.

Instead of taking on the full risk of the underlying index, a buffered ETF helps to reduce some of that risk by providing a buffer to the downside with a cap on the upside over a defined outcome period. Standard buffers range anywhere from 9 percent to 30 percent. Caps, or the most you can earn during an outcome period, range between 7 and 20 percent. The usual correlation is: the deeper the buffer, the lower the cap. An outcome period is the period the underlying index is being tracked. This is typically for one year.

Here's an example. Suppose you want to have exposure to the S&P 500 index, but you want to limit the risk. You decide to invest in a buffered ETF that is linked to the S&P 500. The buffer is 9 percent. The cap is 14 percent, and the outcome period is one year. If over the course of that year the S&P 500 loses 7 percent. Good news: your 9 percent buffer protected you from experiencing that loss. If the S&P 500 dropped 12 percent, you would be down 3 percent. If the market happens to be up 12 percent over the course of a year, you capture the full 12 percent of gains. If the market is up 20 percent, you are still capped at 14 percent. If you want less risk, you can opt for a deeper buffer. Just keep in mind that your cap will likely not be as high. A new outcome period starts the first market day after the previous outcome period ends.

Buffered Exchange Traded Fund Example

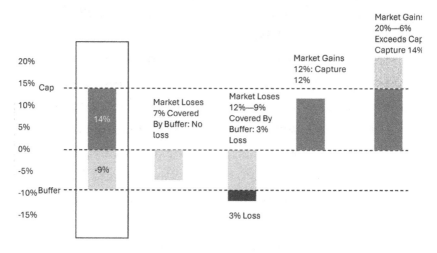

(Hypothetical example shown for illustrative purposes only,
does not reflect any specific investment and is not guaranteed.)

Another benefit of a buffered ETF is that they are intraday liquid. This means you can cash them in for the full amount without penalty anytime the stock exchange is open. Buffered ETFs can be a good option for helping reduce risk in retirement while keeping your liquidity intact. The power to take income when the market is down without compounding losses is a win for many. It's even nice to know that if you get in a pinch and you need to take an oversized distribution, a buffered ETF can provide that flexibility. There are still things you need to keep in mind. Buffered ETFs can be an appropriate option in your retirement portfolio, but you wouldn't want to over-allocate to that position.

To learn more about how buffered ETFs work and how they might benefit you in retirement, please visit thefourhorsemenbook.com.

Fixed Indexed Annuity (FIA)

An FIA is another type of insurance vehicle. Based on my professional experience, it's somewhat of a hybrid between a MYGA, which we discussed earlier, and a buffered ETF. Similar to a MYGA, you purchase this type of annuity from an insurance company instead of at the bank or directly in the market. Unlike a MYGA, however, you aren't guaranteed a set interest rate over a specified period of time. Instead, you have the potential to earn interest each year linked to the performance of an underlying market index, similar to a buffered ETF, and subject to a cap or a participation rate, like a market-linked CD. However, like a MYGA or market-linked CD and unlike a buffered ETF, your principal is one hundred percent protected from any downside.[97] With this type of downside protection, you normally won't find as high of upside potential as with a buffered ETF, but since your interest is linked to the performance of an underlying index, your upside potential could be greater than a MYGA with a fixed rate.

So, how does it work? Since your potential interest is linked to the performance of an underlying index, there will either be a cap or a participation rate involved. We've already seen how caps work with buffered ETF. A participation rate is the percentage of an index's return that is credited to the annuity holder over a set period of time.

Let's go through an example, staying with the S&P 500, which remains the most popular index by far. Say you purchase an FIA with $100,000 and a 10 percent cap, using the S&P 500. If the index is up 7 percent on your annuity contract's anniversary, you'll be credited with $7,000 or 7 percent. If the

S&P 500 was up 15 percent, you'd be credited with just $10,000 or 10 percent since your cap is 10 percent. If instead of a cap, you have a participation rate to the S&P 500 of 50 percent, if the S&P 500 is up 10 percent, you'll be credited with $5,000, half of 10 percent. If the S&P 500 is up 28.88 percent like it was in 2019,[98] you'd be credited with $14,440, 14.44 percent, which is half of 28.88 percent.

In either scenario, if the S&P 500 declined 20 percent in the first year, your $100,000 would remain $100,000. You didn't earn anything, but you didn't lose your principal due to market losses. The power of zero in a negative year in retirement is hard to overstate.

What are the downsides? Just like the other principal-protected vehicles we've discussed, there is a penalty for getting out early. Why is that? When the insurance company receives your money, they purchase investments to back the FIA they issue to you. Many of the investments they purchase to back the policy are long-term investments, so they are dependent on making sure at least some of the money stays long-term. If you exit early, they could be penalized by needing to exercise some of their long-term commitments early as well. The early surrender penalty incentivizes FIA owners to keep more of their money around, so the insurance company won't experience a penalty for an early exit on their end, and this also reinforces the long-term retirement nature of these products. If an early exit is made, the insurance company passes some of the penalty down to the FIA owner, which makes sense.

Common surrender penalty periods for an FIA are five, seven, and ten years. The longer the period, the better the crediting options or growth potential may be, because the insurance company is often able to lock in better rates for themselves if some of your money is expected to be around for an extended period of time. Even with a surrender period, there is still a level of yearly liquidity. Most FIAs provide 10 percent liquidity each year. This means you can withdraw up to 10 percent of the annuity value each year for income.[99] For many, ten percent is plenty of liquidity to provide monthly income in retirement, but due to the constraints, you wouldn't want to allocate too much to this vehicle. It is important to note that the cap or participation rate of an FIA can be changed by the issuing company if the company does not guarantee those rates for the term of the contract. If rates are not locked in initially by the issuing company, it may increase or decrease rates as outlined in the terms of the specific annuity contract. In general, FIAs are not designed to keep up with the long-term performance of the market. Going back to our concept of the three attributes of money, the prioritization of protection means you are giving up a little bit in terms of growth potential and liquidity. In down markets, you'll be glad you have the principal protection, but when the market is up and up big, you still want that piece of your portfolio that can take advantage to the extent possible. That is why finding the right balance of growth, protection, and liquidity is so important.

Speaking of crediting and downside protection, another nice feature of an FIA is the annual reset. Most indexing options for an FIA operate on a twelve-month cycle, crediting interest on the anniversary date of when your FIA was issued.

Let's go through an example. Suppose you purchased an FIA with $100,000 with a 10 percent cap to the S&P 500. In the first year, the S&P 500 was up 15 percent, so your annuity was credited with 10 percent. That $100,000 becomes $110,000 and locks in, but the following year, the S&P 500 is negative 15 percent. You're $110,000 remains $110,000. The annual reset protected your interest credit from the previous year. That's a level of protection you won't get investing directing in the market, a market-linked CD, or a buffered ETF. In the third year, say the S&P 500 is up another 15 percent. You're credited with another 10 percent, and your $110,000 becomes $121,000.

If you had received the direct performance of the S&P 500 over that three-year period based on our example, your $100,000 would be worth $112,412.50 instead of $121,000.

Fixed Indexed Annuity Example

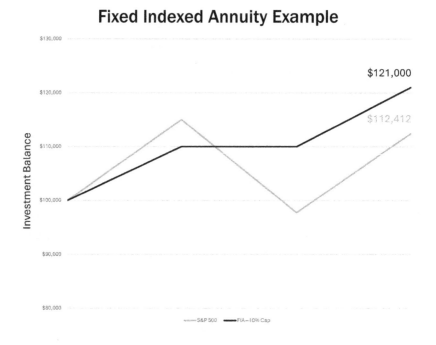

Even being capped at 10 percent, the FIA did better, because it avoided the downside. Again, the expectation is that over time, the FIA will lag the market. The point is that an FIA is a safe place to take income, but there are certain market environments where it will perform better.

I tell families that annuities are just like any other financial product in the sense that there are ones you want to own and ones you don't. There are ones that make sense for one family's situation that don't make sense for another's. It isn't a one-size-fits-all solution. If you've heard horror stories about annuities in the past, it is probably because that family wasn't matched up with the right vehicle for them, or they weren't given a proper explanation of what they were purchasing and why they were purchasing it.

Fees

Lastly, we haven't spent much time discussing fees. There's a chapter on that later. Because of their complexity, protected vehicles can be more expensive, but that doesn't necessarily have to be the case. A buffered ETF may cost a little more than a standard ETF that is tracking an index with no buffer. You're paying for a level of protection not typically offered by a traditional ETF. However, one benefit of an FIA is that, unless you add additional options to the contract, you can purchase an FIA that may not charge you any fee that is directly debited from your account value. All standard fees and charges associated with an FIA are priced into the contract and are reflected in the annuity's terms, such as the surrender charge schedule, the cap and participation rates, payout amounts, and more. Said in more simplistic terms, if the FIA credits 10 percent, that 10 percent is yours. FIAs can be used not only as a protected vehicle but as a way to keep costs down.

Don't get too hung up on fees, though. Many times in life, you get what you pay for. Again, we'll discuss this more when we discuss the horseman of taxes, but it is amazing how some families want to find the cheapest advice possible. Advice from the internet is cheap, but not always the advice I would follow.

One last note on fees before we move on. If you have heard that annuities have high fees, you may be thinking about a variable annuity. I've seen variable annuities with costs as high as 3.5 percent. Not only that, but traditionally, variable annuities invest your funds directly in the market, meaning they may not provide any principal protection. This is not the same as an FIA. There are some variable annuities out there that provide growth potential, with some having caps or participation rates similar to an FIA, but in addition, also provide buffers to the downside similar to buffered ETFs. These types of variable annuities can have comparable fees to an FIA. For the right situation, this can be a legitimate option for the protected money space.

Again, there are hundreds of different insurance companies offering thousands of different products. It's about matching the right solution to the problem.

Just like buffered ETFs and some of the other protected-money options we discussed, we may recommend FIAs in our practice for a portion of the protected money when it makes sense for the specific client situation. However, we find that many families aren't totally aware of how they operate. Bad news travels fast when someone isn't matched with the right investment, so it is sometimes hard to get the right information out there. Once families are equipped with accurate information, they are better able to make informed decisions about how to protect the right portion of their money from market losses while still experiencing growth potential. Many find confidence in knowing that a portion of their portfolio is protected from the downside and opt to have a portion of their assets protected in an FIA.

To learn more about FIAs, how they operate, and if one could be right for you, please visit thefourhorsemenbook.com.

Keeping a portion of the portfolio protected from market losses, whether that be by using T-bills, MYGAs, buffered ETFs, or an FIA, helps to protect families from compounding losses by taking income from their growth money when the market is down. This extends the time available for the money that is allocated toward growth to do what it is supposed to do over time, and that is grow. It isn't about trying to time the market, it is about time in the market.

Unlike the casino where the longer you play the more likely you are to lose, when investing in the market, the longer you invest the more likely you are to win. Having a portion of the money protected helps put time back on your side even if you are in the second half of your financial life. Based on my professional experience, for the thousands of families we have helped to and through retirement, having a portion of the assets allocated to a safe position has proven to be a successful strategy. Not only that, protecting against losses and extending the time your growth money has the potential to grow is a key component of mitigating the horseman of inflation.

Smoothing Out The Ride On The Horseman Of Inflation

Do you remember our first example in this chapter during the discussion on sequence risk when we showed all the retirement money being invested in the market? You started with $1,000,000, and by the end of the tenth year, after withdrawing $40,000 in income plus 3 percent for inflation each year, you only had $883,203 left. You had lost 12 percent of your original investment, and your withdrawal rate went from 4 percent to 6 percent. A scary thought considering that you're only ten years into a potential thirty-year-long retirement, and the horseman of inflation has only just begun to show his true power. At this point, you might be worried about running out of money before you run out of life. If you're not concerned about that, it certainly affects whatever legacy goals you might have.

Later, when discussing the balancing act of the second half of your financial life, we used the same market returns as in the first example, but instead of investing all the money in the market, we positioned 50 percent of it into protected vehicles. This helped smooth out the returns, which is why they look different. Let's assume the two protected vehicles we used for this example were a combination of buffered ETFs and an FIA. Assume the positioning of the money was as follows: 50 percent invested directly in the market for growth, 25 percent invested in buffered ETFs, and 25 percent allocated to an FIA. By keeping a portion of the money protected from market loss, you were able to take the same $40,000 income each year plus a 3 percent increase for inflation. You withdrew a total of $458,555, but instead of ending up with $883,203 at the end of the tenth year, you had $1,049,075.

This is only meant to be an example. This type of strategy might not be the right strategy for you. As always, it is going to depend upon your unique situation, but for many families, having a portion of the money protected from losses means a steadier income stream throughout retirement. It provides the assurance of knowing that their retirement isn't going to be derailed by a bad string of investment years. It helps them to focus on living their lives rather than what the market is doing year over year.

If you would like to see more examples of how protected money can be used to provide security in retirement, please visit thefourhorsemenbook.com.

Sequence Risk							
All Growth				Growth And Safety			
Year	Return	Investment Balance	Income	Year	Return	Investment Balance	Income
0		$1,000,000		0		$1,000,000	
1	-22%	$740,000	$40,000	1	-14.25%	$817,500	$40,000
2	-9%	$632,200	$41,200	2	-4.50%	$739,513	$41,200
3	8%	$640,340	$42,436	3	8.00%	$756,238	$42,436
4	11%	$667,068	$43,709	4	10.75%	$793,824	$43,709
5	7%	$668,743	$45,020	5	7.00%	$804,372	$45,020
6	20%	$756,121	$46,371	6	16.00%	$886,700	$46,371
7	15%	$821,777	$47,762	7	13.50%	$958,643	$47,762
8	-9%	$698,622	$49,195	8	-4.50%	$866,309	$49,195
9	17%	$766,717	$50,671	9	14.50%	$941,253	$50,671
10	22%	$883,203	$52,191	10	6%	$1,049,075	$52,191
Average Return	6%	Total Withdrawals	$458,555	Average Return	6%	Total Withdrawals	$458,555

This is intended for illustrative purposes only and is not indicative of any specific product.

By now, I hope you can truly appreciate how powerful the horseman of inflation is. He's relentless and will stop at nothing to erode the value of your assets, but you can mitigate him with the right planning. How and when you take Social Security and how and when you take your pension, if you are entitled to one, are key components to mitigating the horseman of inflation, but those decisions pale in comparison to how your personal savings are invested for the second half of your financial life.

We discussed how there are plenty of financial professionals out there who are trained to help families accumulate a retirement nest egg. There are fewer out there who are trained to help families create income for life from those assets. If you are nearing or entering retirement, ensure you find an advisor who can help you navigate that complicated task.

All the horsemen ride together. The horseman of longevity increases the power of the other three. Living long is a great blessing, but the longer we live the more opportunity the horseman of inflation has to take hold. This is also true for the other two horsemen, the horseman of taxes, and the horseman of healthcare. Let's move on to the horseman of taxes.

PART III

THE HORSEMAN
OF TAXES

Chapter Nine

TAXES

I recently saw this social media post that sums up a lot of people's frustration with taxes: "Why am I paying taxes on my wage? Then paying sales tax to spend my money? Then paying income taxes on my money they already taxed and paying property taxes after I already paid sales tax on said property?"[100]

This rant could have been posted by any US taxpayer, and it could've kept going. Why am I paying tax on my Social Security when it was a tax to begin with? Why am I forced to pay a higher Medicare premium when I paid the same percentage as everyone else? Why am I paying capital gains tax and net investment income tax on top of my capital gains tax when that money has already been taxed? This list goes on, ad nauseam.

One of your greatest expenses, if not the greatest expense, you will have in retirement is taxes. The horseman of taxes and the horseman of healthcare seem to be duking it out for the top spot, but no matter who wins that battle, we all lose.

The average American will pay $525,037 in taxes throughout their lifetime.[101] That's the average. The average American also has less than $1,000 saved—for retirement or anything else,[102] so chances are if you are reading this book and you've made it this far, you are not the average American. You probably have more saved for retirement than the average American.

That's the good news. The bad news is that if you don't have a plan for how you are going to mitigate your taxes in retirement, you could be on the hook for paying a lot more than the average over the course of your lifetime. Keep in mind that is an individual number, so if you are married, that household figure is $1,050,074. That's a large amount to spend on taxes, and again, that is just the average.

Income Taxes: A Brief History

With some planning, you can dramatically reduce the taxes you pay. But first, let's talk about how we got here in the first place.

The first time the United States started the income tax was in 1861 under President Lincoln when Congress passed the first Revenue Act to help fund the American Civil War. The income tax was later declared unconstitutional by the US Supreme Court in 1895, which meant it would require an amendment to the Constitution for the government to have the power to create an income tax. If only Congress had left well enough alone, but alas, they did not. Congress passed the Revenue Act of 1913, adding the Sixteenth Amendment to the Constitution and resurrecting the federal income tax, giving more strength to the horseman of taxes. We've had an income tax ever since.[103]

Take a look at the chart below. In 1913, when the income tax was reinstated, the top marginal tax bracket was 7 percent.[104] Even if you made $1,000,000 a year back in 1913, the equivalent of $31,850,000 a year today,[105] the highest percentage you would pay on your income was 7 percent. But it didn't take politicians long to realize they could change those numbers. The Sixteenth Amendment opened Pandora's box letting loose the horseman of taxes, and in 1918, shortly after we joined World War I, the top marginal income bracket rose to 77 percent.[106] Wars are expensive, and the government needs more revenue. Therefore, in five short years from the time it became constitutional for the government to impose an income tax, the tax rate increased by a multiple of eleven.

Once the war was over, we saw economic expansion in this country like we had never seen before. Known as the Roaring Twenties, this era and its prosperity allowed tax rates to drop precipitously. Unfortunately, at the end of the decade, we hit an economic wall head-on known as the Great Depression, which started in 1929. This prompted the beginning of entitlement programs like the New Deal and Social Security to help struggling Americans.[107,108] These expensive programs required more revenue to fund them, so taxes started to rise once again. A few years later, after the attack on Pearl Harbor, we joined another war, World War II, and in 1945, we experienced the highest marginal income tax bracket we have ever seen in this country: 94 percent.

We also did something else during World War II at an unprecedented level, and that was deficit spending. Now, don't get me wrong. I'm not saying whether that was good or bad. I'm just reporting the facts. History is a great teacher, which is why it is important to know it. We've all heard the saying if you don't learn from history, you are bound to repeat it.

With all that deficit spending, the United States crossed another threshold for the first time in our nation's history. In 1945, the ratio of debt compared to the gross domestic product (GDP) went above 100 percent for the first time, peaking at 113 percent.[109] To put it more simply, in short, the United States had more debt than the annual amount of income from all the goods and services it produced. It would be like you making $100,000 a year and having $113,000 in credit card debt. That's essentially what the national debt is because there isn't a hard asset like a house backing it up as collateral. Once we crossed that threshold of more debt than income, look how long it took to get tax rates under control. In 1981, the top marginal income bracket was still 69 percent.

Why is all of this important? Again, history is a great teacher. Looking at the past can help us predict potential outcomes in the future. After sixty-six years, in 2014, we surpassed that debt-to-GDP barrier again, and the current national-debt-to-GDP ratio sits at 122.3 percent.[110] Now, look below at where tax rates currently are. Does something seem a little off to you?

Top Marginal Income Tax Rates

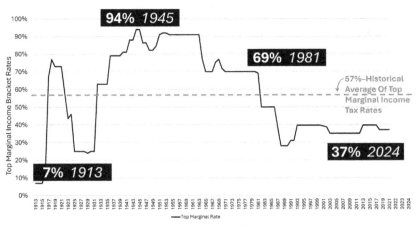

Source: https://taxfoundation.org/data/all/federal/historical-income-tax-rates-brackets/

We've accumulated more national debt than any other time in our nation's history.[111] The cost of servicing that debt has increased, so much so that for the first time, starting in 2024, we spend more paying the interest on the national debt than we do on our national defense and Medicare. The cost of entitlement programs have ballooned to the point that 45 percent of the federal budget is needed just to keep Social Security and health insurance programs like Medicare and Medicaid going. If you tack on an additional 13 percent just to service the interest on the national debt, that leaves less than half for everything else.[112,113] You know, for things like our national defense and military, the Federal Highway Administration, federal pensions, Congress, the IRS, NASA, the FBI, the CIA, etc.

Despite all of that, if you look at our chart one more time, you can see that we remain in a historically low top marginal income bracket. You might be tempted to think, "So what, even if tax rates go up, I'm not in the top marginal income bracket." Don't be fooled. If the top marginal income bracket is going up, your bracket is likely to follow suit, as we will see below. So, what do you think is more likely to happen: (a) the government gets spending under control, or (b) they start taxing us more?

Regardless of which way the political winds blow, history tells us that option (a) is not something we can count on. In fiscal year 2023 (October 1, 2022–September 30, 2023), the federal government collected revenue of $4.44 trillion.[114] It spent $6.13 trillion.[115] That is overspending what it collected by 38 percent.

Most people don't think in trillions, so let's break it down a different way. Let's say last year, your neighbor made $44,400. The only problem is that he spent $61,300. He overspent his income by 38 percent, and he has been doing that for years, for decades even. He's done this so long that he has racked up $343,430 of credit card debt, almost eight times his annual income. What does your neighbor desperately need to do besides learn how to become more financially responsible? If he isn't going to get his spending under control, he needs to increase his income. Unfortunately, our neighbor is the federal government. How does the federal government increase its income? One of the top ways is by finding ways to tax us more.

This leads us to option (b), which is taxing us more. This is already baked into the cake. In 2017, Congress passed the Tax Cuts and Jobs Act, which took effect in 2018. While that permanently reduced the corporate tax rate from 35 percent to 21 percent, making us more competitive on the global stage and leading to economic expansion we hadn't seen in years, the tax cuts the average American saw were temporary. Many

Americans experienced tax reductions, with middle-income earners experiencing tax reductions of 16—26 percent, but again, that was temporary.[116,117] Those tax cuts expire at 11:59 p.m. on December 31, 2025, and we jump back to the brackets we had in 2017. Congress doesn't have to agree on anything or pass new legislation for this to happen. When the old law expires, many families will find themselves jumping from the 12 percent bracket to the 15 percent, the 22 percent to the 25 percent, and the 24 percent to the 28 percent brackets. Some unfortunate families will find themselves jumping two brackets. A 3 percent increase may not sound like much, but moving from the 12 percent bracket to the 15 percent bracket represents a 25 percent increase in your top marginal income tax bracket. That's a significant jump.

Current Tax Brackets Compared To Potential 2026 Brackets

Current Tax Rates Set To Expire On December 31, 2025, At 11:59 p.m.

2025 TAX RATE	SINGLE FILING		2026 TAX RATE	SINGLE FILING
10%	$0–$11,925		10%	$0–$12,170
12%	$11,926–$48,475	↑	15%	$12,171–$49,520
22%	$48,476–$103,350	↑	25%	$49,521–$119,910
24%	$103,351–$197,300	↑	28%	$119,911–$250,060
32%	$197,301–$250,525	↑	33%	$250,061–$543,700
35%	$250,526–$626,350	↑	35%	$543,701–$545,920
37%	$626,351 or more	↑	39.6%	$545,921 or more

2025 TAX RATE	MARRIED FILING JOINTLY		2026 TAX RATE	MARRIED FILING JOINTLY
10%	$0–$23,850		10%	$0–$24,335
12%	$23,851–$96,950	↑	15%	$24,336–$99,035
22%	$96,951–$206,700	↑	25%	$99,036–$199,760
24%	$206,701–$394,600	↑	28%	$199,761–$304,470
32%	$394,601–$501,050	↑	33%	$304,471–$543,700
35%	$501,051–$751,600	↑	35%	$543,701–$613,245
37%	$751,601 or more	↑	39.6%	$613,246 or more

Source: https://www.bankrate.com/taxes/tax-brackets/#tax-bracket-2025
https://www.bankrate.com/taxes/2017-tax-brackets/

Adding insult to injury, with our recent bout of inflation, we will also likely experience another phenomenon we discussed in our section on the horseman of inflation, and that is bracket creep. We have seen significant inflation in recent years. If wages begin to increase over the next several years to balance out the equation, tax brackets are not likely to keep up. This means the wage increase will likely be taxed at a higher rate as you either enter a new tax bracket entirely or progress through the current bracket you are in more rapidly.

With the Trump administration returning to office, we may see the current tax cuts extended, but the writing is on the wall. Taxes are probably going up unless something else radically changes. It's my opinion that it's not a matter of if. It's a matter of when.

Option (b), taxing us more, is clearly on the table. The likelihood is the government will be forced to make cuts at some point, option (a), but I believe that higher taxes are almost certainly on their way sometime in the future.

It doesn't necessarily stop with increasing tax brackets either. Yes, there is tax risk, but there is something else that doesn't get discussed nearly enough, and that is legislative risk. What happens if the government changes the rules on us in the middle of the game? This has already started to happen, as we will examine in further depth below, but first, have you ever been told you should defer your taxes because you will be in a lower tax bracket in retirement? What guarantee is there that this might be the case? Could it be possible for your taxes to be higher in retirement? Aside from an increase in tax brackets, there are several reasons why this might be more likely than you realize.

When you enter retirement, the goal for most people is not to live on less or reduce your standard of living. No one comes to us saying, "Spencer, we are looking forward to tightening our belts in retirement. We're going to decrease our spending, avoid travel, and never leave the house again." That is never the conversation.

For the families we serve, the goal is to live as well, if not better, than before they retired. It certainly isn't to reduce their income. They may even spend a little extra in those early years of retirement, traveling and doing some of the extra things they couldn't do while working and saving for their golden years. In fact, we often encourage it and build a plan to support that goal. We have a saying in our office. "You are never any younger, healthier, or freer than you are today." We want families to be able to get out and do the things they want to while they can still do them.

We'll revisit the chart below when we get to the horseman of healthcare, but as you can see, a typical family will spend the most through the first few years in retirement. Then, spending decreases some before increasing again, mainly due to end-of-life care.

Annual Average Household Spending By Age

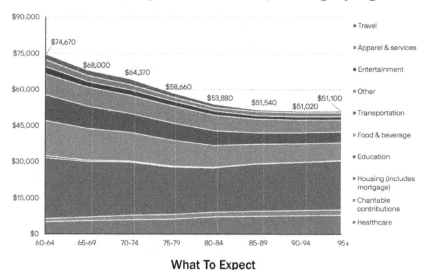

What To Expect

Average spending declines from the early part of retirement, then tends to flatten out. Those at older ages tend to spend less on all categories except healthcare and charitable contributions. Those who live to the oldest ages may have costs related to long-term care.

Source: J.P. Morgan Asset Management, based on internal select data from JPMorgan Chase Bank, N.A. and its affiliates (collectively "Chase") including select Chase check, credit and debit card and electronic payment transactions from January 1, 2017 to December 31, 2023. Check and cash distribution: 2019 CE Survey; J.P. Morgan Asset Management analysis. Information that would have allowed identification of specific customers was removed prior to the analysis. Other includes: tax payments, insurance, gambling, personal care and uncategorized items. Asset estimates for de-identified and aggregated households supplied by IXI, an Equifax Company; estimates include all financial assets except employer-sponsored plans and do not include home equity. Additional information on J.P Morgan Asset Management's data privacy standards available at https://am.jpmorgan.com/us/en/asset-management/mod/insights/retirementinsights/gtr-privdisc/. Retired households receive retirement income only, including Social Security, pension and/or annuity payments.

On top of potentially spending a little more during those early years, another reason why your taxes may be higher in retirement is having fewer deductions. Your children may be grown up and out of the house. The house is likely paid down or paid off, so you aren't getting an interest deduction, and you may not be giving as much charitably once your paycheck stops. Fewer deductions can mean more in taxes.

A third reason for increased taxes is that if you are currently married, you are benefiting from the married filing joint brackets, but what happens when one spouse passes away? The surviving spouse is now a single filer subject to the much smaller single-filer brackets. If you don't plan for it, a surviving spouse can be living on less income but paying more in taxes than they ever have before. We'll talk more about that in a moment.

Here's a simple example. In 2025, a married couple with $80,000 of taxable income is in the 12 percent tax bracket. If one of them becomes a surviving spouse now subject to the single-filer brackets, even with 20 percent less income, $64,000, they would be in the 22 percent tax bracket. With a 20 percent loss of income, their top marginal income tax bracket jumped 83 percent.

A fourth reason why your taxes may be higher in retirement is those pesky required minimum distributions (RMDs) that you have to take from your pretax retirement accounts. In case you didn't know it already, at a certain age, the IRS requires you to take money out of your IRA, 401(k), 403(b), Thrift Savings Plan, or any such pretax retirement accounts. These are accounts where you didn't pay taxes when you were putting money in, so when you take it out, you owe tax not only on what you put in but all the growth as well. By forcing you to take distributions, the IRS is forcing you to pay those taxes you were once able to defer. If you don't take the required amount out, there is a 25 percent penalty, and you still owe the income taxes on the amount you didn't receive because it was penalized. Currently, you must start taking RMDs at age seventy-three.

Here's the kicker. RMDs are structured in a way that they are likely to increase each year based on the predetermined IRS calculations. This means you will have to withdraw more and more money each year only to owe more tax. Those distributions don't stop or get smaller if you are a surviving spouse filing as a single filer. They just keep getting bigger. Therefore, your taxes in retirement may not just be higher. Without good planning, they could increase every year.

Legislative Risk

One risk often overlooked in discussions about taxes is legislative risk. What happens if the government changes the rules in the middle of the game? Unfortunately, we have begun to see that happen recently.

Changing the rules in the middle of the game is what we all experienced when Congress passed the Setting Every Community Up for Retirement Enhancement Act in 2019, otherwise known as the SECURE Act. Congress then passed the Securing a Strong Retirement Act in 2022, also referred to as SECURE Act 2.0. In my opinion, after years of reviewing financial legislation, Congress has a habit of using names that sound great but often have little to do with the actual legislation.

So, what did the SECURE Act and SECURE Act 2.0 do? Collectively, they raised the RMD age from seventy and a half to seventy-three. The age will rise to seventy-five in 2033, so if you were born in 1960 or later, your RMD age is seventy-five. The larger concern with these pieces of legislation is how pretax retirement accounts are inherited, especially when it comes to a non-spouse beneficiary.

If part of your plan was to leave money to your children, and you don't want an unnecessary amount eaten away by taxes, you have some tax planning to do. Unless very specific requirements are met, children who inherit retirement money can no longer stretch payments out over their lifetime, effectively stretching out the tax liability. They must now deplete the accounts within ten years.[118]

Suppose a child inherits $1,000,000 of pretax money. They would have to take a distribution of $100,000 a year, plus interest, to have the account depleted by the end of the tenth year. Could that potentially bump them into a higher tax bracket? Absolutely, it could, and in my opinion, I would argue the government is banking on it. To make matters worse, the children who inherit these pretax dollars are likely to inherit them in their fifties and sixties during their peak earnings years. They may be making more money than they ever have before in their careers and now have to take substantial distributions from their inheritance, which could propel them into even higher brackets.

As demonstrated by the SECURE Act and SECURE Act 2.0, raising taxes isn't the only tool the government has at its disposal to raise the amount of taxes you will be liable to pay. They can change the rules, and through simple rule changes, the government can dramatically increase your tax bill. This is legislative risk. There's an estimated $35 trillion in retirement accounts across the United States.[119] I can't think of a larger untapped bucket of money the government has an incentive to go after than your retirement savings. You'd better believe they're aware of that, hence the changes we have seen and the coming changes we may be in for.

There seems to be an ongoing shift in Washington's attitude regarding retirement accounts. When Congress passed the Revenue Act of 1978, which paved the way for the 401(k) plan, the common thread seemed to be the idea of giving Americans a chance to save for retirement on their own. Instead of depending only on Social Security or a pension plan, instead of placing your faith in the government or your company to take care of you in your old age, you could put money into a tax-advantaged vehicle to take care of yourself later in life. This represented a true alignment with the American ideal of independence.

In my opinion, the sentiment seems to be, "Look at those greedy Americans. Look how much they have saved for retirement. That's more than they need. They're just being selfish. We could put that money to better use." We saw Washington tip their hand in one of the first iterations of the Build Back Better Act that was introduced to Congress in 2021. The original bill was a $3.5 trillion spending bill with $2.9 trillion in new taxes to help pay for it. Where were the new taxes going to come from? If you guessed a large portion coming from your pre-tax retirement accounts, you guessed right. On the fact sheet for the bill published by the House Committee on Ways and Means, in Subtitle I, Part 3, Subpart A–Limitations on High-Income Taxpayers with Large Retirement Account Balances, it reads, "To avoid subsidizing retirement savings once account balances reach very high levels, the legislation creates new rules for taxpayers with very large IRA and defined-contribution retirement account balances."[120]

What were the new rules? They force those the government has deemed to have saved too much for retirement into a two-tiered RMD system. You would have to take your regular RMD, and then an assessment would be made about how much "excess" you have in your pretax retirement accounts. Once the "excess" is determined, you may be forced to take a distribution of up to 50 percent of the excess. How much money is too much money in your pretax retirement accounts? We don't have the answer to that, and whatever amount gets determined is likely to change as the government gets more and more hungry for those tax dollars.

It's hard to overstate how significant this shift is, and forcing a 50 percent distribution of the "excess" can be a significant number. The bottom line is that this is designed to force you to take more money out of your pre-tax retirement accounts so more taxes can be collected. A larger distribution means adding more income to the highest marginal income tax bracket you fall into or potentially pushing you to a higher bracket all together. It can increase the amount you are forced to pay in capital gains tax by becoming subject to the net investment income tax (NIIT), which is an additional 3.8 percent tax on your capital gain tax rate. It can also increase the amount you pay on Medicare premiums by forcing you into a higher income-related monthly adjusted amount (IRMAA). We'll talk more about IRMAA later on.

Thankfully, this provision was not passed as part of the bill that morphed into the Inflation Reduction Act of 2022, which was signed into law by President Biden on August 16, 2022, but I believe that nothing ever dies in Washington. It just gets put on a shelf for later use, and wouldn't you know it, this same type of proposal was made part of the Biden Administration's budget for 2025. While it is not likely to be included in the Trump administration's budget, this type of proposed legislation represents a fundamental shift in thinking when it comes to retirement accounts. In my opinion, instead of congratulating Americans on a job well done as they sacrificed to build wealth for themselves and their families, Washington looks on with lustful eyes.

When it comes to legislative risk, it is important to know not only what has been passed but also how it affects you. It's important to know what is being discussed. The provision in the failed Build Back Better bill is just one example of legislative changes that could affect you in the future.

Chapter Ten

THE THREE TAX BUCKETS

emember the three attributes when it comes to investing your money? In Chapter 8, we discussed the attributes of growth, protection, and liquidity and how finding the right balance is crucial to creating a successful retirement plan. When it comes to taxes, there are three ways to think about money. I like to refer to them as buckets.

The Tax-Deferred Bucket

The first bucket, the one that most people use to save for retirement, is the tax-deferred bucket. We've already discussed this bucket quite a bit. This bucket is filled with all the money that you have yet to pay taxes on. When you placed money in this bucket, you deferred paying the tax on what you put in and the growth of the money until a future date. That future date comes when you start taking money from that bucket. Those distributions, including what you put in and the growth, are subject to income tax.[121] The types of accounts that fit into the tax-deferred bucket include 401(k)'s, 403(b)'s, 457 plans, Thrift Savings Plans, IRAs, pensions, and many more. We use the accounts in this bucket to kick the proverbial tax can down the road until a future date.

Here's the kicker. Based on everyone's lived experience, it's safe to wager that taxes are likely going up in the future. If that's true, why would we defer taxes if we believe we're going to be subject to higher tax rates later? Yet that's what so many people do, placing money in, what I believe, is possibly the worst asset you could own if taxes are going up.

Think about your own retirement accounts. Are most of your assets in a pretax account? If so, you may have some work to do to help mitigate and minimize your impending tax liability. We'll get into some strategies for this in chapter 11.

The Taxable Bucket

The second bucket is the taxable bucket. All the stuff you pay taxes on as you go is in this bucket. One example is an individual or joint brokerage account on which you pay capital gains. It could also be a savings, checking, money market account or a certificate of deposit where you pay tax on the interest each year. It could be a business or a revocable family trust. Essentially, you get tattletale letters (tax notices) on these accounts each year in a tax form like a Form 1099 or Schedule K-1 stating that you made money and you owe the tax.

The Tax-Free Bucket

The third bucket is the tax-free bucket. These are accounts that allow the money inside them to grow tax-free, and then you take the money out tax-free.

Roth IRA

The number one tax-free account available today is the Roth IRA. The idea of the Roth IRA was first introduced in 1989, but it wasn't until 1998 that legislation was passed that brought it to bear. Named after the main architect, Senator William Roth, the Roth IRA allows individuals the opportunity to put after-tax money into an account that can grow tax-free instead of tax-deferred. That means anytime you go to take money out of this account in the future, as long as you follow the rules, you receive the funds without tax.[122]

Roth 401(k)

Another investment vehicle inside the tax-free bucket is the Roth 401(k). Here's something to consider: 88 percent of 401(k) plans offer a Roth 401(k) option.[123] Rather than the employee contributing their funds to the traditional 401(k), where they would grow tax-deferred, employees can contribute to a Roth 401(k), where the funds can grow tax-free.

Keep in mind that the tradeoff for using a Roth IRA or Roth 401(k) instead of a traditional IRA or 401(k) is that, unlike with a traditional plan, you are not excluding your contributions from your current income when you contribute to the Roth option. There is no tax deduction on the front end. Instead, you are allowing the money to be taxed prior to going into the Roth account. Once the money is in the account, it can grow tax-free.

If you believe your taxes will be higher in the future, it might make sense to pay the tax now when the amount is small and allow it to grow tax-free. That way, you get to access a larger sum of money without owing any tax. The alternative is to delay or defer paying the tax now while the amount is small and pay potentially higher taxes on a larger sum of money in the future.

In 2021, despite most employers providing a Roth 401(k) option, only 28 percent of workers who participated in a 401(k) contributed to a Roth 401(k).[124] Why is that? Because employees are often unaware that the option exists and that the benefit is not explained. Now that you know the benefits, if you are still working, you may want to check and see if this option is available and if it makes sense for you to take advantage.

There is a cap on how much you can contribute to a Roth IRA and Roth 401(k) account in a given year. For 2025, the contribution limit for a Roth IRA is $7,000 if you are under the age of fifty. If you are fifty or older, you are allowed a catch-up contribution of $1,000, so the total contribution amount to a Roth IRA for those fifty and over is $8,000. This contribution limit also applies to traditional IRA accounts.

For 401(k)'s, the contribution limit is $23,500 if you are under the age of fifty. If you are fifty or older, you are allowed a catch-up contribution amount of $7,500, making your total allowable contribution $31,000 if you are over the age of fifty.

Starting in 2025, If you are age 60, 61, 62, or 63, your allowable catch-up contribution is $11,250. Making the maximum contribution to a 401(k) or other employer-sponsored plan, such as a 401(b), 457 plan, or Thrift Savings Plan, $34,750. This was part of the Securing a Strong Retirement act that was passed in 2022.

If you turn age 60 in 2025, your allowable catch-up contribution is $11,250, but if you turn age 64 in 2025, your catch-up contribution amount is $7,500. The ages for the additional catch-up contribution are 60, 61, 62, and 63.

Cash Value Life Insurance

Since the government views Roth IRAs as being such a good deal, they place restrictions on who can contribute directly to them. Sometimes, high-income earners have a difficult time getting money into a Roth IRA. Maybe you don't have that issue, but your employer is one of the few that doesn't offer a Roth 401(k) option. Maybe you've already maxed out your Roth IRA or Roth 401(k) for the year, which has left you looking for an alternative tax-free savings vehicle.

In any of those cases, that is where cash value life insurance may make sense. Life insurance primarily functions to provide financial protection to your beneficiaries in the event of your death. It can cover essential needs such as income replacement, debt payment, and final expenses. Certain types of life insurance, like whole or universal life policies, also offer the added benefit of cash value accumulation, which can grow tax-deferred. Additionally, there are scenarios where you can take policy loans or withdrawals on a tax-advantaged basis. However, it's important to weigh these benefits alongside the policy's costs, potential impacts on the death benefit, and your overall financial plan. Consulting with a qualified tax advisor or financial planner can help determine if this aligns with your financial goals.

Life insurance is, first and foremost, a vehicle designed to provide a death benefit once you pass. Properly structured life insurance can allow for tax-free growth inside the policy. Life insurance does involve insurance-related fees and charges. Also, it requires medical and often financial underwriting to qualify, so it is important to work with someone knowledgeable to decide whether it is an appropriate fit. Cash value life insurance offers additional features that appeal to many high earners looking for tax benefits. The cash that accumulates inside a properly structured life insurance policy not only has the potential to grow tax-free but can also be used for tax-free income in the future. The best part is that there are no IRS contribution limits. Any income withdrawn from the policy is deducted from the policy's death benefit and cash values. These can cause the policy to lapse or require additional premiums to keep it in force, depending on how much you take out, which is why it's crucial to work with an experienced insurance professional to carefully structure and manage the policy.

For example, you might prioritize your savings for retirement by maxing out your Roth IRA and Roth 401(k) first. It's only once you've done that when cash value life insurance often makes more sense. Another potential benefit of a cash value life insurance policy is some of the long-term care benefits it can provide. This is something we will dive deeper into when we discuss the horseman of healthcare, but with nearly 70 percent of those turning age sixty-five today expected to need at least some form of long-term care services throughout their remaining years, having a little protection in your back pocket can be extremely valuable.

A properly structured cash value policy can allow the cash value to grow on a tax-deferred basis. Additionally, policy loans and withdrawals, if managed correctly, can potentially be accessed tax-free.

Health Savings Account (HSA)
Another tax-free savings vehicle is a health savings account (HSA). To contribute to one of these accounts, you have to

be a part of a high-deductible health insurance plan. The beauty of this account is you get a tax deduction when you make a contribution, and as long as you use the funds for a qualified medical expense, distributions come out tax-free, including what you put in and any growth. Normally, you can't use the funds to pay for healthcare premiums, but that changes if you are on Medicare. You are allowed to use your HSA funds tax-free to pay for your Medicare premiums. We will delve further into HSAs in chapter 14. An HSA can be an effective vehicle to take with you into retirement, and it is one that is often overlooked and underutilized.

As you begin to think about your money in terms of the three types of retirement accounts—the tax-deferred bucket, the taxable bucket, and the tax-free bucket—you'll likely notice something glaring. In my experience, the majority of families find that the buckets look something like the below example. The tax-deferred bucket holds most of their assets. The taxable bucket may have a little in it, and if you are fortunate to have a tax-free bucket, there are typically only drops.

The Three Tax Buckets

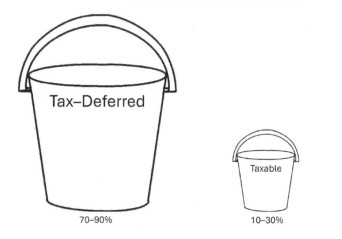

Tax–Deferred

70–90%

Taxable

10–30%

Tax–Free

<1%

The potential problem with the tax-deferred bucket is it represents both what may be a large future tax liability and impending legislative risk, and the longer it takes for you to begin to mitigate it, the worse it may get. We need to consider shifting money from the tax-deferred bucket over to the tax-free bucket in a tax-efficient way.

Here, we come back to the concept of getting the right money in the right place at the right time. You may not be able to completely eliminate the tax burden of your tax-deferred bucket, but anything you can do to reduce it means keeping more money in your pocket and in your retirement accounts. More money for you means a higher likelihood of success in retirement. Even if you can simply work to get your buckets relatively even, it's possible, depending on your situation, to save tens or even hundreds of thousands of dollars in taxes not only over your lifetime but over the life of your retirement accounts.

Now that you know the potential power of the horseman of taxes, it's time to talk about the strategies that can help you better mitigate him. In the next section, we will begin to discuss several strategies, and I'll finish with an example of what it might look like in practice.

Chapter Eleven

TAX STRATEGIES

A hypothetical couple, let's call them Jeff and Susan, are worried about how taxes were going to affect their retirement plan. Life happened, and they did not have as much savings as they wished. The good news is that they had not touched their IRAs. Was there anything they could do?

How could they get more of their money moved into the (mostly) tax-free bucket? Here are four possibilities.

Strategy Number One: IRA Conversion

One of the common strategies for mitigating the tax burden in retirement is a Roth conversion. A Roth conversion is a taxable event and should be done with caution. Financial decisions can have a domino effect, as we discussed before. That shouldn't keep you from making smart choices. You just don't want to be surprised by a domino falling you didn't expect.

A Roth conversion is when you take money from the tax-deferred bucket from a traditional IRA, 401(k), or other employer-sponsored plan, pay the tax on that money, and move it over to the tax-free bucket into a Roth account. This can be a Roth IRA, Roth 401(k), or some other Roth employer-sponsored plan account.[125]

The most basic concept is this. Let's assume you are in the 22 percent tax bracket, and you're confident that you will be in the 25 percent tax bracket in the future once the current tax law expires.

If you are in the 22 percent tax bracket now, and you'll be in the 25 percent tax bracket in the future, might it make sense to take some money out now and pay 22 percent? Again, pay attention to the other financial dominos that may fall, but let's say you could convert $50,000 without knocking over any other dominos or sending yourself into another tax bracket. You take $50,000 from your pretax retirement account in the tax-deferred bucket, pay a federal tax of 22 percent or $11,000, and move the remaining funds ($39,000) into a Roth IRA in the tax-free bucket where all future growth is tax-free. The immediate impact is that you paid 22 percent or $11,000 in federal tax instead of waiting until a time you would owe 25 percent or $12,500 in federal tax, a difference of $1,500.

Maybe $1,500 doesn't excite you too much. That's OK. The benefits don't stop there. Remember, the money can now grow tax-free instead of tax-deferred, so when you did that conversion, you also removed all the future tax liability on the growth of that money. You'll no longer be growing the IRS's share of your money. You'll just be growing your money. Depending on how tax rates change and how much you decide to convert, thousands in taxes can be saved.

For a video example, please visit, please visit us at thefourhorsemenbook.com.

When you reduce the tax-deferred bucket, future RMDs will be less. For those who are married, if one spouse passes away, they have more options on where they can take money to reduce taxes as a single filer, and if money is inherited by your children or a non-spouse beneficiary, that money is inherited tax-free, eliminating the taxes collected on that portion of the inheritance.

Is there a specific age at which you should do a Roth conversion? I would argue that any time is a good time because, in the long run, it can provide clear tax benefits. That being said, there are strategic times when it is more advantageous to do a Roth conversion.

Here's a fun example. Imagine the market is like a Slinky toy. It regularly expands and contracts. Sometimes, the Slinky is stretched out, and the market is at all-time highs. Sometimes, the market is compressed when we are going through periods of decline. This rhythm of expanding and contracting can create great opportunities for Roth conversions.

Here's a hypothetical example going back to 2020. Let's assume you had a $100,000 IRA at the beginning of 2020. The Slinky was stretched out. The S&P 500 posted a 31.49 percent total return in 2019.[126] We were well into all-time highs, and then COVID-19 hit. The S&P 500 dropped 34 percent to its low in 2020. Your IRA was suddenly worth $66,000. This is not wonderful news, but it would be an excellent time to convert to a Roth at a market low.

Converting at this point, what would you pay tax on? You would pay on $66,000 instead of $100,000. When the market fully recovered from that low by August of that year, you gained all that growth tax-free. When the S&P 500 continued to rise and finished up 18.40 percent on the year, not only did you gain back all the money tax-free, but you also gained back all the tax you had to pay for the conversion.

Instead of finishing the year with a tax-deferred account worth $118,400, you finished the year with a tax-free account worth $118,400. If you assume tax of 25 percent, you would have had to pay $16,500 to convert the $66,000, so your net at the end of the year would be $101,900. If you still owe 25 percent to the IRS in your tax-deferred account worth $118,400, that's a net of $88,800, which is a difference of $13,100.

While this may be an extreme example, it illustrates what a specific downturn can present. In my professional experience, every market dip is a potential opportunity for doing a strategic Roth conversion that has the potential of saving you thousands of dollars in taxes over the life of your retirement accounts.

Speaking of maximizing conversions, there are two ways to pay the tax on your conversion. One way to pay the tax on the funds being converted, and likely the optimal way, is for you to pay it from a source outside of your IRA. That way if you had $100,000 in your tax-deferred IRA, you now have $100,000 in your tax-free Roth IRA. That was the strategy in our previous example, because the tax on the $66,000 was paid from an outside fund, it left the full $66,000 invested and available to receive the entire upside of the market. That strategy isn't always possible, because not everyone has $16,500 laying around to devote to taxes as a moment's notice. Don't worry. Another way to pay for the tax on a conversion is from the conversion itself. This was the first example given when we discussed converting the $50,000. You'll want to consider each option carefully and run the numbers to make sure the conversion still benefits your long-term tax strategy.

Both ways may work to help reduce your tax liability and increase your tax-free earning potential. The concept is simply to take your least tax-advantaged money—the tax-deferred bucket and the taxable bucket—and use it to create your most tax-advantaged money, your tax-free bucket.

Sometimes, families think they are too old to start a Roth IRA, that they've waited too long to reap the benefits. I haven't found that to be the case yet, especially if part of your plan is for your IRA money to outlast you.

Earlier, I mentioned dominoes that can fall when making financial decisions. Here are a few to pay attention to regarding a Roth conversion.

A Roth conversion can:

- Increase your marginal tax bracket
- Increase taxes on Social Security
- Increase Medicare premiums or reduce a healthcare subsidy
- Increase capital gains tax
- Cause you to become subject to the NIIT

These are just a few of the dominoes that you can accidentally knock over if you don't know what to look for. Fortunately, you may be able to minimize these with proper planning.

Strategy Number Two:
Qualified Charitable Distribution

Another strategy is called qualified charitable distribution (QCD). Let's assume you are charitably inclined and give to your church regularly, but you don't have enough deductions on your tax return to itemize. This means that you don't get to recognize the tax benefit of your giving. Now, don't get me wrong. I know you don't give for the tax benefit, but if there is a tax benefit to gain, I believe that is part of being a good steward of your money.

To do a QCD, you have to be age seventy and a half, so you might put this strategy in your back pocket for a later date if you aren't at that age, but once you reach age seventy and a half, you can transfer money directly from your pretax IRA to a qualified charity of your choice. The beauty of this strategy is that the money that comes from your pretax IRA is not taxable to you, nor is it taxable to the charity. It completely cuts out the IRS. The current limit on how much you can transfer as a QCD in a given year for 2025 is $108,000, so for most families, that is plenty of room to work with.[127]

Remember our discussion on RMDs? At a certain age, the IRS is going to start forcing you to take money out of your pretax retirement accounts whether you need the money or not. A QCD counts toward your RMD amount. If you are forced to take more than you need, and you are charitably inclined, a QCD can be a great strategy to help reduce how much of the RMD shows up on your tax return. If you are going to give to charity, you might as well do it in a tax-efficient way.

Note: the QCD has to go directly from your IRA to the charitable organization. It can't pass through your hands first. Otherwise, the money is taxable to you.

Strategy Number Three: Donor-Advised Fund

What if you are charitably inclined, under the age of seventy and a half, and can't itemize your deductions? Is there a solution for you? Yes, there is. This would be a donor-advised fund (DAF). In this example, let's assume a married couple gives $10,000 a year to charity and has minimal deductions to itemize on their tax return. Because of this, they take the standard deduction of $30,000 for 2025. They get to deduct $30,000 from their taxable income as a free gift from the government, but what about the $10,000 they gave to charity? Well, since $30,000 is more than $10,000, they're going to deduct the standard deduction of $30,000. There is no tax benefit to the $10,000. How can we fix this?

Instead of giving $10,000 a year, what if they could lump several years of giving together? In our family's case, they had the ability to do this, and they transferred $50,000 into a DAF. One of the benefits of a DAF is that you don't have to disperse all the money at once. It can grow inside the account tax-free and be dispersed when you are ready.

Gifts made to the DAF are irrevocable. Once the gift is made, it's made, but this allows you to deduct the entire amount of the gift in the year it was given. In this case that's $50,000. Now, instead of being stuck with the standard deduction of $30,000, our family can deduct the entire $50,000 gift plus whatever other deductions they may have.

By giving $50,000, our family gave five years of donations at once, so in year one, they will get to itemize their deductions. In years two through five, they will take the standard deduction, and once we get to year six, they can decide if they want to repeat the strategy. Just like with a QCD, if you plan to give the money away anyway, why not do it in a tax-advantaged manner?

Just like with our Roth conversion strategy, where not everyone has a large pile of money lying around to devote to taxes, most families don't have a pile of money lying around to give away, even if it is to their favorite charity. That's OK. Here's another potential strategy for using a DAF.

Let's assume you have a highly appreciated stock. Maybe you bought Apple at the perfect time. If you sell the stock, you're likely going to owe capital gains tax on that sale. A DAF can accept stock transfers. Let's go back to our $50,000 example, but this time, pretend it is all in Apple stock. You bought the stock for $10,000, and now it is worth $50,000. If you sell it, you're recognizing a gain of $40,000. At a 15 percent capital gains tax rate, that is $6,000 owed to the IRS. Instead, you transfer that stock over to your DAF. Now, instead of owing $6,000 in capital gains tax, you get to deduct $50,000 from your income. If that $50,000 is taxed at 25 percent, that's $12,500 you saved on taxes. With the additional $6,000 in capital gains tax you avoided, that's an $18,500 swing.

This still requires that you are charitably inclined and were going to give away $50,000 over the course of several years anyway. If you aren't charitably inclined, you would likely still like to have the $50,000 minus the difference in tax owed. Even still, there are additional benefits to this strategy. Keep in mind our financial dominos idea. This type of donation has the potential of dropping you into a lower tax bracket because you will have the ability to itemize deductions and lower your overall taxable income.

Whether you are or aren't charitably inclined is not always important when looking at different strategies that involve a charitable organization. If you are interested in mitigating your taxes and keeping more of your money, the use of certain estate planning strategies that utilize charities can help you accomplish those goals. In the end, you can potentially accomplish your goals, reduce taxes, and retain more of your money, and charity is a bonus. This can be done through certain trusts. I'm not an attorney, but if you have a large estate with significant money in your tax-deferred bucket, exploring these options together with your financial advisor and attorney can be extremely worthwhile. The tax savings must be significant for this to make sense because the setup and ongoing maintenance can be expensive.[128]

Strategy Number Four: Establish A Trust

One last strategy I want to discuss involves the use of a trust. This applies to those who own a business or large physical asset like an office building, apartment complex, or series of homes. If you have been successful in building a business or in real estate of some sort, there is a significant chance that you may face a large tax consequence when you go to sell your business(es) or property(ies).

Rick And Betty

While it may be impossible to eliminate the taxes you will owe, there may be ways to help you reduce them. Here's a hypothetical illustration. Rick and Betty are married and are both doctors. Early on in their practice, they decided to build their own medical building. They built it twenty years ago, and it cost them a total of $850,000 to build it. The building is now worth $2,850,000. Even with the improvements, because of depreciation, we'll still assume that their cost basis—the amount that isn't taxable when they sell their buildings—is $850,000, for example purposes.

If they were to sell the building outright, that would equate to a capital gain of $2,000,000, enough to force them from a 15 percent capital gains tax rate to a 20 percent capital gains tax rate and make them subject to the 3.8 percent NIIT. Assuming no other income for this example, if they were to sell the building, it would cost them a total of $425,420 in taxes. What if there was a way to stretch those payments out a bit and recognize that capital gains more slowly? Fortunately, such a way exists.

Before selling their building, Rick and Betty transferred the title to a trust. The trust then sold the building and received the entirety of the assets from the sale ($2,850,000). Instead of paying Rick and Betty all at once, the trust was set up to pay them in a series of installments. In our example, it paid them out over five years, allowing them to only recognize a portion of the capital gain each year. This kept them in the 15 percent capital gains bracket and reduced the amount that would be subject to NIIT. Ultimately, their total tax liability would be $261,563 for a total tax savings of $163,857 or 38.5 percent.

Let's take it a step further. What if Rick and Betty didn't need the proceeds from the sale of their medical building? They are both successful doctors and had plenty saved for retirement. Their ultimate goal is to leave the money from the sale of their medical building to their two daughters as an inheritance. Again, if they simply sell the building, assuming no other income, they are going to owe $425,420 in taxes on money they want to leave for their children. Fortunately, there could be another way. Before selling the building, they can transfer ownership to a charitable remainder trust.[129]

Now, when the building is sold, the proceeds go to the charitable remainder trust. How much tax is due at the time of the sale? Zero, and the entire $2,850,000 is able to be invested inside of the trust. The minimum distribution rate that must be taken is 5 percent each year, so the starting income is $142,500. Rick and Betty don't need the income. They want an inheritance for their two daughters, so they use the income to purchase a life insurance policy on both of their lives called a second-to-die policy. This means both of them must pass before the death benefit is paid. The annual income from the trust was used to purchase a life insurance policy with a death benefit of approximately $4,275,000, which will pass tax-free to their two daughters.

Now, we have eliminated the initial capital gains tax and provided an even larger tax-free inheritance to their children. Even better, the donation made to the charitable remainder trust may be able to be used as a charitable deduction to reduce Rick and Betty's adjusted gross income, reducing their taxable income.

How These Strategies Can Work Together

As we close our section on the horseman of taxes, I want to walk you through how I've seen the use of some of these strategies play out in the real world.

John And Lisa

I want to tell you about a hypothetical couple, John and Lisa. John and Lisa had done everything they thought was right, everything they were told to do to prepare for a successful retirement. They are now seventy-five years old, have been retired for over ten years, and married to each other for over forty. Imagine them as two of the most amazing people you could ever meet.

John worked many years for a local business that specialized in food products, while Lisa worked as a nurse. When John retired, he started collecting around $27,000 in Social Security a year. Lisa worked part-time throughout part of her career to be more involved in their children's lives when they were younger, which led to her Social Security benefit being slightly less, so when she started collecting Social Security, her benefit came to $20,500 a year.

Both of them contributed to defined-contribution plans through their employers while they were working. John had a 401(k), and Lisa was part of a 403(b) plan. John and Lisa are both savers and did quite well in their plans. At retirement, John had $700,000 in his 401(k), while Lisa had $450,000 in her 403(b).

Based on what Social Security provided for them, they only needed $30,000 a year from their retirement accounts to maintain their standard of living and do everything they wanted to do. Before taxes were taken out, their combined income in retirement was $77,500 (John's Social Security $27,000, Lisa's Social Security $20,500, and investment income $30,000).

That was when they started their retirement. Fast forward ten years, and with cost-of-living adjustments to Social Security, John and Lisa are receiving around $58,600 a year in Social Security benefits. They only need around $40,000 from their investments to maintain their standard of living and to keep up with inflation, but a couple of years ago, they turned RMD age. Even though they only needed $40,000 from their investments, they were forced to take out a little over $74,500, $34,500 more than they needed. This is shown in Table A.

Because of that RMD, their income is $133,000 instead of $98,600. Our tax code is a progressive system. This means the tax burden increases with income. Here's what it looks like for John and Lisa. First, they get to take their standard deduction. This is the amount of income the government allows you to exclude from your taxes. Essentially, that money is tax-free. The standard deduction for married filing joint in 2024 was $29,200. John and Lisa are also both over sixty-five, so they get to take an additional deduction of $1,550 each bringing their total deduction to $32,300. Social Security is taxed a bit differently, so we only have to worry about $49,800 or 85 percent of it being subject to tax.

Here's where we are so far. Taxable Social Security of $49,800 and taxable investment distribution of $74,500 for a total of $124,300. Now subtract the standard and over age sixty-five deductions of $32,300, and we have a taxable income of $92,000. That puts John and Lisa in the 12 percent tax bracket.

As we mentioned, however, we have a progressive tax system, so some of the money ($0–$23,200) is taxed at 10 percent, and the rest ($23,201–$92,000) is taxed at 12 percent for a total tax liability of $10,576.

Keep in mind that prior to the Tax Cuts and Jobs Act of 2017, their tax bill wouldn't be projected to be $10,576. It would be $12,583 based on a taxable income of $92,000, a 19 percent increase.[130] That is potentially what we can look forward to next year, and as we discussed, it will likely get worse.

Table A – John And Lisa Tax Example

$133,000 – Total Income		2024 TAX RATE	MARRIED FILING JOINTLY
$49,800–Taxable Social Security		10%	$0–$23,200
$74,500–RMD		12%	$23,201–$94,300
$124,300–Income		22%	$94,301–$201,050
-$29,200–Standard Deduction		24%	$201,051–$383,900
-$3,100–Over 65		32%	$383,901–$487,450
$92,000–Taxable Income		35%	$487,451–$731,200
$10,576–2024 Tax Liability		37%	$731,201 or more
$12,583–2026 Projected Tax Liability			

Time's ticking, but do you know what the Tax Cuts and Jobs Act of 2017 didn't fix or what the next tax bill won't fix, regardless of what political party happens to be in office? What if something happens to John or Lisa?

Unfortunately, the story doesn't get any better for John and Lisa, especially for Lisa. One beautiful summer day, John is out golfing with his buddies when they come upon the first par three of the day. John steps up to the tee box. He does a little wiggle and hits a smooth seven-iron right at the pin. He can't believe his eyes as his ball one hops and rolls right into the cup. It's John's first ever hole-in-one. He's so excited that he throws his club, jumps up and down in celebration with his friends, and suddenly, John takes a big gasp for air. John's ticker gives out right there. He suffers a massive heart attack and is gone before the ambulance arrives.

What happens to Lisa? What income will she lose? Social Security will increase her benefit to match what the highest recipient was receiving for a married couple, but the rest of their Social Security benefit goes away. At this time, John was receiving $33,400 a year from Social Security, which was more than Lisa's, so Lisa kept the $33,400 but lost the rest. Fortunately, Lisa doesn't need quite as much to live on, with a little less needed for healthcare, clothing, food, and other miscellaneous expenses. Plus, they were already used to cross-saving the extra money they were forced to take out because of their RMDs. For the sake of this story, let's assume Lisa is going to be just fine on income.

Lisa has a different problem. She has a tax problem. Lisa is no longer married, filing jointly. The following year, she will be a single filer under the tax code. Here's what the numbers look like now, the year after John has passed.

Lisa's Social Security income is now $34,235, because of a cost-of-living adjustment. Her RMD is now $80,000 because she is another year older. So, her total income is $114,000. Still, only 85 percent of Social Security is subject to tax, which is $29,000, as shown in Table B. That, combined with her RMD of $80,000, brings her total to $109,000. Her standard deduction is now $15,000 as a single filer in 2025, and she only gets one over-age-sixty-five deduction of $2,000 as a single filer in 2025, which brings her total deduction to $17,000. This makes her taxable income $92,000. Wow, does that look familiar? That is the same taxable income from the year prior when John was still alive, but how is the tax code treating Lisa now?

Before, when John was alive, they were in the 12 percent tax bracket. Now that John has passed, Lisa is a single filer subject to the single filer brackets. Her top marginal income bracket is now 22 percent. Some of the money is taxed at 10 percent and some at 12 percent, before the rest is taxed at 22 percent. This means her total tax bill is $15,154. Her total income is reduced by 14 percent, but she is paying 43 percent more in taxes. Based on what the situation might look like after the current tax law expires and we return to the 2017-style brackets, Lisa's tax bill would then be $17,493.

Table B – Lisa Tax Example

$114,000 – Total Income	2025 TAX RATE	Single
$29,000–Taxable Social Security	10%	$0–$11,925
$80,000–RMD	12%	$11,926–$48,475
$109,000–Income	22%	$48,476–$103,350
-$15,000–Standard Deduction	24%	$103,351–$197,300
-$2,000–Over 65	32%	$197,301–$250,525
$92,000–Taxable Income	35%	$250,526–$626,350
$15,154–2025 Tax Liability	37%	$626,351 or more
$17,493–2026 Projected Tax Liability		

The situation only gets worse as Lisa's RMD grows each year, forcing her to pay more and more in taxes, and Lisa still has another problem. She has a Medicare problem.

Here is yet another example of how the horsemen ride together. We will talk more about Medicare when we discuss the horseman of healthcare, but since Lisa's modified adjusted gross income (MAGI) is above $106,000 (remember, her income before taxes and deductions was $114,000), she will have to pay more for her Medicare Part B and Part D premiums. She can file for a one-time exemption since she had a qualifying life-changing event (the passing of her husband). While that helps her for the current year, it doesn't help her for future years.

As shown in Table C, instead of paying $185.00 a month for Medicare Part B based on the 2025 table, Lisa will have to pay $259.00 a month based on the 2025 table. As shown in Table D, instead of paying just the plan premium for Medicare Part D, she will have to pay an additional $13.70 a month based on the 2025 table.[131]

Table C - Medicare Part B 2025 Premium Table

Beneficiaries Who File Individual Tax Returns With Modified Adjusted Gross Income:	Beneficiaries Who File Joint Tax Returns With Modified Adjusted Gross Income:	Income-Related Monthly Adjustment Amount	Total Monthly Premium Amount
Less than or equal to $106,000	Less than or equal to $212,000	$0.00	$185.00
Greater than $106,000 and less than or equal to $133,000	Greater than $212,000 and less than or equal to $266,000	74.00	259.00
Greater than $133,000 and less than or equal to $167,000	Greater than $266,000 and less than or equal to $334,000	185.00	370.00
Greater than $167,000 and less than or equal to $200,000	Greater than $334,000 and less than or equal to $400,000	295.90	480.90
Greater than $200,000 and less than $500,000	Greater than $400,000 and less than $750,000	406.90	591.90
Greater than or equal to $500,000	Greater than or equal to $750,000	443.90	628.90

Table D - Medicare Part D 2025 Premium Table

Beneficiaries Who File Individual Tax Returns With Modified Adjusted Gross Income:	Beneficiaries Who File Joint Tax Returns With Modified Adjusted Gross Income:	Income-Related Monthly Adjustment Amount
Less than or equal to $106,000	Less than or equal to $212,000	$0.00
Greater than $106,000 and less than or equal to $133,000	Greater than $212,000 and less than or equal to $266,000	13.70
Greater than $133,000 and less than or equal to $167,000	Greater than $266,000 and less than or equal to $334,000	35.30
Greater than $167,000 and less than or equal to $200,000	Greater than $334,000 and less than or equal to $400,000	57.00
Greater than $200,000 and less than $500,000	Greater than $400,000 and less than $750,000	78.60
Greater than or equal to $500,000	Greater than or equal to $750,000	85.80

Is that fair? Is it fair that Lisa is living on 14 percent less income and paying 43 percent more in taxes? Is it fair that she is living on 14 percent less income and subject to paying 47 percent more in Medicare Part B and Part D premiums? Absolutely not. Can it be fixed? Not as easily as it could be after John hits the hole-in-one, but what if Lisa owned a silver DeLorean, the one straight out of *Back to the Future*, that gave her and John the opportunity for a do-over?

How might they have planned to do things differently?

Now, John and Lisa are alive and well, both sixty-five again, and are planning for retirement. They're still going to get the same from Social Security. They still need $30,000 from their investments plus a little more each year to help combat inflation, but the planning doesn't stop there. Instead of just letting their tax-deferred money ride, increasing their future tax liability as it grows, they decide to do something about it.

After doing some tax planning, they decide they are comfortable taking an additional $70,000 out of their tax-deferred bucket each year, paying the tax, and moving it to their tax-free bucket, where it can now grow tax-free. This additional distribution will put them in a higher top marginal income tax bracket, but they also know that this is already going to happen in the future based on their projected RMD. Additionally, it will only get worse if one of them ends up as a single filer if one spouse predeceases the other.

To illustrate this, we need to make some assumptions. We'll assume 25 percent of the money they convert goes to paying the tax on the conversion, and the rest goes to their tax-free bucket, a Roth IRA. We will also assume that all accounts continue to grow by 7.5 percent. By doing a conversion each year for eight years before hitting their RMD age, they will have converted over $622,000 if they increase the amount a little each year to take advantage of tax brackets expanding a little each year.

Under this scenario, they pay the tax, and $466,500 is placed into their tax-free bucket, which, now, at age seventy-three, is worth over $648,000. This is money that they will never have to pay tax on again, nor will their children. Plus, there is still $932,000 in their tax-deferred bucket, and we'll assume they stopped converting once they reached their RMD age of seventy-three.

At age seventy-five, God forbid, if something happens to John, Lisa's tax situation now looks radically different. Lisa is still going to get $34,235 from Social Security. As shown in Table E, her RMD is $34,000, not $80,000, because there is less money in her tax-deferred bucket after doing the Roth conversions. However, she needs more than $34,000 from her investments to maintain her standard of living. That's OK. She can take an additional $5,500 from her tax-deferred bucket for a total of $39,500. This brings her total income to $73,735. If she needs more than that, she can supplement the rest from her tax-free bucket to stay in the 12 percent bracket.

In this new scenario, less of Lisa's Social Security is subject to tax now that she isn't forced to take as much from her tax-deferred bucket, meaning she receives more of her Social Security tax-free. That, combined with her deductions of $17,000, brings her taxable income to $46,225, keeping her within the 12 percent tax bracket.

Now, Lisa's tax liability is $5,309, a 65 percent reduction in taxes from the previous scenario where no tax planning was done, and Lisa won't be subject to the higher Medicare Part B and Part D premiums. Not only has she mitigated the horseman of taxes, but she is well on her way to mitigating the horseman of healthcare as well.

Table E – Lisa's Do Over Tax Example

$73,735 – Total Income	2025 TAX RATE	Single
$23,725–Taxable Social Security		
$34,000–RMD	10%	$0–$11,925
$5,500–Investment Income	12%	$11,926–$48,475
$63,225–Income	22%	$48,476–$103,350
-$15,000–Standard Deduction	24%	$103,351–$197,300
-$2,000–Over 65		
$46,225–Taxable Income	32%	$197,301–$250,525
$5,309–2025 Tax Liability	35%	$250,526–$626,350
	37%	$626,351 or more

That's only the beginning for John and Lisa. By reducing their tax liability early on, they can potentially save tens or even hundreds of thousands of dollars in taxes throughout their retirement. Instead of their RMDs pushing them into higher tax brackets in the future, they retain more control over their tax situation. They reduce the likelihood they will be forced to pay more in Medicare premiums due to the additional forced income a higher RMD would create for them.

They've also protected themselves from future rule changes. Right now, up to 85 percent of Social Security can be subject to tax. No matter what your income, you get 15 percent tax-free. But what happens if the government raises the limit to 100 percent? They have the flexibility of limiting how much of their Social Security is subject to tax. If new tax laws are passed that increase John and Lisa's tax brackets, their tax-free money is protected. The tax has already been paid. If the government disallows the use of Roth IRAs in the future, they will likely have grandfathered accounts that still produce tax-free income for them.

What about the money after John and Lisa have both passed? John and Lisa have three children, John Jr., Beth, and Susie, and they want to leave an inheritance for them. Think about the SECURE Act and how it changed the way IRA money is inherited. John and Lisa's children will be subject to the ten-year rule, meaning they need the IRA withdrawn by the end of the tenth year. If John and Lisa had never done a single Roth conversion, and all the money was left as a pretax IRA to their children, each child would need to take out $50,000 a year, plus interest, to have the account depleted within ten years.

Could that force the children into a higher tax bracket when they are likely to inherit that money in their fifties or sixties, when they are hitting their peak earning years in their careers? Could it force them to pay more taxes on their Social Security income if they are collecting? Could it force them to pay more in Medicare premiums if they are over the age of sixty-five? The answer to those questions is yes. In my opinion, I would argue that is exactly what the government is hoping will happen to many Americans. Why were the rules changed in the first place? It was to induce more taxes.

By using Roth conversions, John and Lisa increased the amount of money that would be passed on tax-free to their children, and they reduced the potential negative outcomes listed above. All that is accomplished with eight years of Roth conversions, but John and Lisa don't have to stop there. They could continue to implement strategic Roth conversions even after they started taking their RMDs. The benefits could continue to compound. Potentially, some families can even get themselves to the point where they no longer owe any federal income tax, and none of their Social Security is taxable. Fewer taxes means you have more of your money available to you to spend.

Now, it's possible that John and Lisa could lose out if the tax brackets are reduced in the future. Then, it is possible that the Roth conversions were not beneficial as they were executed when rates were higher. After considering the risk versus reward, John and Lisa decided that they were more likely to experience higher tax rates in the future, and they especially felt that way for their children at the time they would inherit the money.

As the law currently stands, we are expected to hit higher tax rates starting in 2026 when the current law expires. Congress can simply let the old law expire, but what happens if and when Congress is forced to take action? What happens when our overspending neighbor from Chapter 9 has no choice but to raise his income level by raising tax brackets?

All the way back in 2008, in an analysis titled "The Long-Term Economic Effects of Some Alternative Budget Policies," the Congressional Budget Office predicted that tax rates would have to more than double in the future and laid out a three-bracket system of 25 percent, 63 percent, and 88 percent.[132] I don't think this is that far-fetched at all. These kinds of rates have existed in this country's past. We have been kicking the deficit-spending can down the road for quite a while. I believe it's only a matter of time.

It is hard to put into words just how important I believe making sure you are taking steps to mitigate your future tax liability is. It is hard to show the full benefit mathematically because none of us knows exactly how high taxes could go in the future. Just know this: the higher the taxes, the more valuable mitigating your future tax liability becomes.[133]

Taxes On Social Security

It's been mentioned several times already, but you are likely going to have to pay taxes on your Social Security. Yes, it was a tax to begin with, but the government will tax you on it again. Based on the history of Social Security, it was never intended to be taxed. From the time that Social Security was enacted in 1935 to the time the first check was received in 1940, all the way to 1983, Social Security was never subject to tax, meaning beneficiaries received their Social Security tax-free. All that changed when Congress passed the Social Security Amendments of 1983 Act during the Reagan administration to address both short-term and long-term financing problems facing the program.[134]

The rates for how Social Security is now taxed were set in 1983 and became effective in 1984, and they have never been adjusted for inflation. That simply means that more and more of the Social Security income of the beneficiaries has become subject to tax as time has rolled on.

As shown in Table F, if you're single and your modified adjusted gross income (MAGI) is above $25,000, up to 50 percent of your Social Security is going to be subject to tax. If it's over $34,000, up to 85 percent of your Social Security is going to be subject to tax.

If you are married filing joint and your MAGI is above $32,000, up to 50 percent of your Social Security is going to be subject to tax, and if your MAGI is above $44,000, up to 85 percent of your Social Security is going to be subject to tax.

Table F – Tax On Social Security

Single		Married Filing Joint	
Up To 50% Taxable	$25,000 MAGI	Up To 50% Taxable	$32,000 MAGI
Up To 85% Taxable	$34,000 MAGI	Up To 85% Taxable	$44,000 MAGI

The point I want you to take home is these are not large numbers. You don't need to stress out about trying to figure out how to calculate the tax on your Social Security. You just need to be aware that the threshold for your Social Security being taxed is not a high one, which means your Social Security will likely be, at least partially, subject to tax.

Remember, under current law, even if you are in the highest threshold for your Social Security being taxed, you are still going to receive 15 percent of it tax-free. Social Security is not a tax-free source of income, but because not all of it is taxable, it is a tax-advantaged source of income. You can use this to your advantage on your quest to overcome the horseman of taxes.

Here's why this is so important to take into consideration when deciding on how and when to take your Social Security benefit. None of the money you withdraw from your pre-tax retirement accounts—your tax-deferred bucket—is coming to you tax-free. By using your least tax-advantaged money first, not only are you potentially maximizing your Social Security benefit over your lifetime to mitigate the horseman of inflation, you are also growing a larger tax-advantaged income stream to help you mitigate the horseman of taxes.

Getting this decision right alone has the potential of saving you tens of thousands of dollars in retirement.

The Golden Window Of Tax Planning

The golden window of tax planning, as I call it, usually takes place during one's early to mid-sixties. It could happen a little sooner or a little later, but typically, it's during this period that the greatest opportunity to reduce your future tax liability exists, especially if you have prepared in advance.

When you are newly retired, you are likely to have no or little employment income. You may not have started drawing Social Security, and you are not required to take distributions from your pretax retirement accounts. You may have fairly low taxable income, and if you have prepared in advance for this time, you have a nice cash reserve built up.[135]

The key to maximizing this window of opportunity is to prepare in advance. By having a cash reserve built up, you can fund your lifestyle while delaying Social Security and reducing your tax liability. Utilizing this window effectively is just another way to help mitigate the horseman of taxes.

The Horseman Of Taxes

Experience tells you the horseman of taxes is powerful, but with the right tools and strategies, you can help manage him.

Not having a plan for how you are going to mitigate and minimize taxes in retirement is like going on a long journey and ignoring the check engine light. You might be OK in the short term, but eventually, you could run into problems. You won't be happy when you do, so it's better to start taking care of it now.

PART IV

THE HORSEMAN OF HEALTHCARE

Chapter Twelve

HEALTHCARE AND AGING

Welcome to the horseman of healthcare. Like the other horsemen, the horseman of healthcare does not ride alone. The horseman of longevity increases the likelihood that you will spend more on healthcare throughout retirement. The longer you live, the more you are likely to spend on healthcare, and the cost isn't linear. Remember our chart from before? Healthcare costs are one of the few categories that is projected to increase throughout the entirety of retirement.

Healthcare costs may stay relatively low throughout the beginning of your retirement but are likely to increase exponentially as you age. Increasing healthcare costs is the horseman of inflation's playground. Since 2000, inflation on the price of medical care has outpaced the inflation on all consumer goods and services by 35.2 percent.[136] Your $100 for goods and services in 2000 now costs $186.10, but your $100 medical bill costs more than $221.30.

Annual Average Household Spending By Age

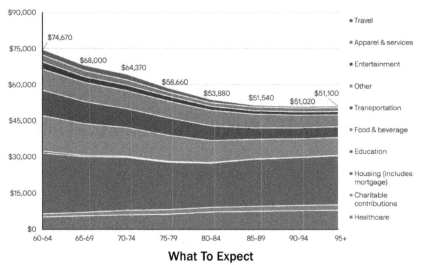

What To Expect

Average spending declines from the early part of retirement, then tends to flatten out. Those at older ages tend to spend less on all categories except healthcare and charitable contributions. Those who live to the oldest ages may have costs related to long-term care.

Source: J.P. Morgan Asset Management, based on internal select data from JPMorgan Chase Bank, N.A. and its affiliates (collectively "Chase") including select Chase check, credit and debit card and electronic payment transactions from January 1, 2017 to December 31, 2023. Check and cash distribution: 2019 CE Survey; J.P. Morgan Asset Management analysis. Information that would have allowed identification of specific customers was removed prior to the analysis. Other includes: tax payments, insurance, gambling, personal care and uncategorized items. Asset estimates for de-identified and aggregated households supplied by IXI, an Equifax Company; estimates include all financial assets except employer-sponsored plans and do not include home equity. Additional information on J.P Morgan Asset Management's data privacy standards available at https://am.jpmorgan.com/us/en/asset-management/mod/insights/retirementinsights/gtr-privdisc/. Retired households receive retirement income only, including Social Security, pension and/or annuity payments.

According to a Fidelity study done in 2023, an average sixty-five-year-old can expect to spend approximately $157,500 in healthcare and medical expenses throughout retirement.[137] Naturally, a married couple aged sixty-five can expect to spend twice that, or $315,000, throughout their retirement. Delegating as much as several hundred thousand dollars toward healthcare is bad enough. Still, that estimate excludes long-term care services, which have the potential of adding hundreds of thousands or more in healthcare costs throughout retirement.

Just like with all the other horsemen, if you are going to effectively mitigate the horseman of healthcare, you need to have a plan in place.

How Will Your Healthcare Be Covered?

Most families are aware of the federal health insurance program known as Medicare, but most won't become eligible for Medicare until they turn sixty-five. With the average retirement age at sixty-three, how will you be covered if you retire before you are eligible for Medicare? Fortunately, you have a couple of options.

Retiring Before Sixty-Five

If you work for a larger employer, one option that you will likely have available is the ability to use the health benefit provisions of the Consolidated Omnibus Budget Reconciliation Act, or COBRA. This option allows you and your spouse, if applicable, to continue being a part of your employer's plan for an additional eighteen months after you have retired, but there's a catch.

Most employers plan to pay a portion of the cost of health insurance for their employees and potentially even their spouses or families. Under COBRA, you become responsible for 100 percent of the cost of insurance. Instead of you paying a portion of the premium amount each month and the employer paying a portion of the premium, you are responsible for the whole thing. Plus, the employer is allowed to charge an additional 2 percent to cover administrative costs, so using the COBRA option can be expensive.

If you are married and your spouse isn't retiring, you could explore hopping onto the plan provided by the other employer. This is likely to be less expensive than COBRA, but you will want to compare prices and coverage to avoid surprises like being out of network or having no coverage on services for which you've grown accustomed to having coverage.

If neither of those options is appealing or feasible, your third option is to shop for a private plan. I recommend doing this with the help of a knowledgeable independent health insurance agent. Typically, an independent health insurance agent will gather your information, get an understanding of the type of coverage you're looking for, and provide several quotes from various insurance companies. They shouldn't be pushing one particular insurance company, but instead will likely match you up with the company that is the right option for you. Even better, there is generally no cost that you pay the agent. The agent is paid a commission by the insurance company to match you up with their plan.

The Health Insurance Marketplace at HealthCare.gov is another resource. Here, you can plug in some of your relevant information and get an idea of what a plan might cost you.

It's possible that if you don't do any preplanning and you retire before the age of sixty-five, you will end up paying more for your healthcare than you did before you retired. If you are in a situation in which your healthcare costs will increase for a couple of years prior to being eligible for Medicare, ensure that is included in your financial plan.

If your plan accounts for the increase in premium cost and it doesn't affect your probability of success in retirement, there is no reason to panic. However, unexpected expenses can be financially costly, which is why you want to consider the increase in healthcare costs.

Minimizing Taxable Income Every Other Year

If your goal is to retire before age sixty-five and you plan for it, there may be a strategy that you can use to help lower the cost of your healthcare premiums. This was the case for a hypothetical couple, Michael and Trisha. In 2023, Trisha had already retired. Michael was sixty-two years old and knew he wanted to retire at the first of the year when he would only be sixty-three.

After taking into consideration their assets, current income from his employment, and their overall retirement plan, they decided to take extra money from their accounts in 2023. Some of this was taken from IRA accounts where tax was owed. They were able to stay in their current tax bracket. Some funds were taken from taxable accounts where capital gains tax was owed. Once this was done, they had all the money they needed to maintain their standard of living throughout 2024.

The only income they showed in 2024 was minimal taxable interest, dividends, and capital gains, along with Trisha's Social Security income. When they signed up for a healthcare plan, this allowed them to qualify for a subsidy to reduce their monthly premium amount, reducing their total monthly cost of insurance down to a couple of hundred dollars, less than what they were paying under Michael's employer plan. It did cost them a little extra in tax initially, but the plan is estimated to save $18,000 in premium costs in 2024, which far exceeds the extra they paid in taxes.

If you plan to retire at sixty-one, this strategy can be used on an every-other-year basis. For example, you take everything you need to live on for two years in year one. This allows you to show little income in year two. In year three, you take twice what you need again; you won't qualify for a subsidy this year, but this allows you to show little income for year four. After year four, you qualify for Medicare at sixty-five, and the strategy is complete.

This isn't a strategy that makes sense for everyone. It is truly dependent upon available assets and how distributions may affect your tax rates and other expenses, but it could be a feasible option for some families.

Chapter Thirteen

UNDERSTANDING
MEDICARE

As we have seen in exploring the four horsemen, there are no free rides. The same is true for Medicare. While Medicare users report satisfaction with quality of care of well above 90 percent, there are no caps on out-of-pocket costs on Parts A and B.[138] Understanding what is covered, the various facets of Medicare Parts A, B, C, and D, and how to mitigate your personal cost burden will help keep the horseman of healthcare at bay. We'll go into more detail about each part of Medicare throughout the chapter. For now, just know that Medicare Part A covers your hospital and facility costs. Medicare Part B covers your doctor's visits and doctor's costs, but Medicare Part B only covers 80 percent of those costs. The Medicare beneficiary covers the remaining 20 percent. Since the remaining 20 percent can be quite expensive, many families opt for what is known as Medicare Part C, Medicare Advantage plan, or a Medicare Supplemental plan, which is sometimes referred to as a Medigap plan because it covers the gap not covered by Medicare Part B. Both Medicare Advantage plans and Medicare Supplemental plans are designed to help provide payment for the 20 percent that Medicare Part B does not cover. Lastly, Medicare Part D covers your prescription drug costs.

A Medicare Short Story

My maternal grandparents live as though the world ends at the border of our hometown. Most of their adult children and grandchildren live locally, and they don't have much desire to travel. When they signed up for a Medicare plan, they both decided to go with a Medicare Advantage Plan. They both had parents who lived well into their nineties and remained in good health until they died peacefully in their own homes. They were healthy, and they liked the idea of low or zero monthly premiums and only paying for the care they needed when they needed it.

Roughly three years into retirement, my grandfather looked at my grandmother and said, "You know what, we haven't been anywhere since we retired. Let's take a trip to Florida for a long weekend," so they did. They even stayed in a hotel right on the beach.

One night, while on the trip, my grandfather looked at my grandmother and said, "Baby, I'm feeling some Mexican food tonight," so they went to get Mexican food. My grandfather, as he is known for doing, ordered the spiciest thing he could find on the menu, and it was delicious.

They enjoyed the rest of the evening and finished with a walk on the beach before returning to the hotel to call it a night. At three a.m., my grandfather woke up with one hand on his chest and the other hand searching for my grandmother. He was convinced he was having a heart attack.

My grandmother called 911, and they were quickly transported to the local hospital, where they ran an EKG—normal. They checked his cardiac enzymes to see if he had a heart attack—normal. The nurse walked in and handed my grandfather a cup with some white, chalky liquid in it, and he took it. It was Mylanta. Twenty minutes later, my grandfather was good to go.

The good news is, he didn't have a heart attack; he was just dealing with the worst bout of indigestion he had ever had. The bad news is he didn't have a heart attack, which, because the hospital he went to was not in network, means he is personally responsible for all costs associated with the visit. Emergency visits are covered out of network under a Medicare Advantage Plan, but it must be an emergency. Indigestion is not an emergency, so when he got the bill for being out of network, he was at risk for a real heart attack.

The mistake my grandparents made wasn't picking a Medicare Advantage Plan. In reality, that plan worked out really well for them. Their mistake was not being fully aware of what was covered under their plan and not taking appropriate action when they decided to travel for vacation. Maybe there was a hospital in their network that was close by that they could have gone to instead, or maybe they could have purchased some additional insurance to protect them while they traveled. They could have taken either or both of those steps if they were better informed about their plan.

My parents, on the other hand, travel quite a bit, and unfortunately, my father doesn't have the best family history regarding health concerns. When it was time to sign up for a Medicare plan, both my parents opted for a Medigap (Medicare

Supplement Insurance) plan to supplement Parts A and B. Medigap helps them cover the copays and deductibles that they are exposed to with Parts A and B. They know they can switch to a Medicare Advantage Plan in the future if they desire. For now, the monthly premiums are affordable for them; they like the flexibility the Medigap plan provides, and they don't have to worry about high unexpected medical bills if, for some reason, they have an unexpected health occurrence.

Charting Your Medicare Story

Most individuals who reach the age of sixty-five are eligible to receive Medicare benefits. If you are still working at the age of sixty-five and are already covered under a qualified health insurance plan, you can delay signing up for Medicare until you retire or your qualifying coverage ends. Normally, an employer-sponsored healthcare plan from your job will count as qualifying coverage, but it doesn't hurt to double-check. Using COBRA or having a private healthcare plan does not count as qualifying coverage, and you will want to sign up for Medicare.

If you are covered under your employer plan, you may choose to delay starting Medicare because Medicare can often be more expensive than what your employer is providing for you.

For now, let's assume that you are turning age sixty-five and you won't have qualifying coverage. Therefore, you'll be signing up for Medicare. If you've already started your Social Security benefit, you will automatically be enrolled in Medicare Part A, and you will just need to ensure you sign up for Medicare Part B. If you haven't started drawing Social Security, you will need to be sure to sign up for Medicare Part

A and B, also known as Original Medicare. You can sign up by going to ssa.gov and clicking on "Sign up for Medicare" under the heading that says "Apply." You don't have to have already started your Social Security benefit to be eligible for Medicare.

You can enroll in Medicare Part A and Part B three months before or after turning sixty-five. If you don't have qualifying coverage, be sure to apply on time; otherwise, there can be significant penalties. The penalties for late sign-up to Medicare Part B and Part D are lifetime penalties that never go away. Why the stiff penalties? If everyone waits until they need the care to start paying the premiums, the penalties provide sufficient deterrent or offset losses for those who do sign up late.

Medicare Part A

Medicare Part A covers your facility costs such as a hospital stay, skilled nursing facility stay, home healthcare, or hospice care. Part A does not cover long-term care expenses. It does cover a skilled nursing facility stay if extended rehab is needed from a hospital stay, but recovery must be part of the expectation.

There is no premium due for Part A if you or your spouse has forty qualifying quarters under Medicare. There are four quarters to a year: January–March, April–June, July–September, and October–December. If you earn $1,730 in a given quarter, that counts as a qualifying quarter.[139] That equates to $6,920 a year, so most Americans who have worked throughout their adulthood will qualify without paying a premium. If the forty-quarter threshold is not met, monthly premiums can be as high as $505 a month.

There are additional costs to Part A, like deductibles and per-day costs, depending on how long you stay at a particular facility and what type of facility it is. This can be covered by a Medigap or Medicare Advantage Plan, which we will discuss later in this chapter.

Medicare Part B

Medicare Part B covers doctor visits and outpatient services. There is a premium for Medicare Part B coverage. Monthly premiums range from $185.00 to $628.90 per individual per month in 2025. If you are married, you would owe two monthly premiums. Premium payments are typically automatically deducted from your monthly Social Security payment. If you haven't started drawing Social Security, or your monthly check isn't large enough to cover your Part B premium, you must make a separate payment.

How much you pay in Medicare Part B premiums is determined by your modified adjusted gross income (MAGI). Your MAGI is your adjusted gross income (AGI) with some stuff added on, like the nontaxable portion of Social Security and tax-free interest from municipal bonds, among other items. For most retirees, their MAGI is relatively close to the same as their AGI, so it usually isn't a big concern. You can easily find your AGI on your tax return where it says "adjusted gross income."

Pay attention to your MAGI because it determines your Medicare Part B premium cost. Doing strategic Roth conversions, as we explored in the horseman of taxes, can help you avoid bumping yourself into a higher Medicare Part B premium bracket—another example of how the horsemen ride together. The adjustment that Medicare makes to your premium based on your MAGI is known as the income-related monthly adjusted amount (IRMAA), and you can find the various levels in the accompanying chart.

It can make sense, depending on the numbers, to still do a Roth conversion even if it bumps you into a higher Medicare Part B bracket. The increase in your Medicare bracket will only last a year unless you continue to bump yourself into a higher bracket each year. The benefit of the tax savings compounds for life, as we discussed previously. The biggest thing is ensuring you aren't surprised by an increase in Medicare premiums.

You'll notice that the chart states that what you pay in Medicare Part B premiums is based on what happened two years prior. For example, what you pay in 2024 will be based on your MAGI in 2022. Keep this in mind. If you start Medicare when you are sixty-five, what you pay in Part B premiums will be based on the tax return for the year you turned sixty-three, so if you plan to off-load a large asset or do a Roth conversion, it may make sense to do it before then. I bring this up for several reasons.

Table G – Medicare Part B 2025 Premium Table[140]

Beneficiaries Who File Individual Tax Returns With Modified Adjusted Gross Income:	Beneficiaries Who File Joint Tax Returns With Modified Adjusted Gross Income:	Income-Related Monthly Adjustment Amount	Total Monthly Premium Amount
Less than or equal to $106,000	Less than or equal to $212,000	$0.00	$185.00
Greater than $106,000 and less than or equal to $133,000	Greater than $212,000 and less than or equal to $266,000	74.00	259.00
Greater than $133,000 and less than or equal to $167,000	Greater than $266,000 and less than or equal to $334,000	185.00	370.00
Greater than $167,000 and less than or equal to $200,000	Greater than $334,000 and less than or equal to $400,000	295.90	480.90
Greater than $200,000 and less than $500,000	Greater than $400,000 and less than $750,000	406.90	591.90
Greater than or equal to $500,000	Greater than or equal to $750,000	443.90	628.90

Let's say you are a landlord. You've invested in some rental properties or maybe even some apartment buildings. You didn't mind being a landlord while you were working. Maybe that even becomes your full-time job, but now that you plan to retire, you don't want the burden of having to be responsible for that property or properties anymore. You want to be able to travel and leave your worries behind, not worry about getting a call concerning a leaky roof, running toilet, or the water heater going out. If you sell those properties prior to the year you turn sixty-three, you won't have to worry about an increase in your Medicare Part B premiums. Keep in mind that this counts for your spouse, too, if you are married. If you are married and filing joint, the increase in MAGI affects both your premium amounts.

There are other financial dominoes to pay attention to. Imagine you have several properties that you want to sell, but you are over the age of sixty-three. Being strategic about when you sell each property can help keep you in a lower premium bracket. It can also help reduce the amount of income and capital gains tax you pay as well.

Maybe you have been awarded several stock options through your employer, or you have stock that has a large gain that you want to diversify away from. These types of situations can create large capital gains that will affect your MAGI as well.

As with all plans, we want to be looking forward to the future. Remember our conversation about RMDs? If you don't plan in advance, your RMD could push you to higher premium brackets depending on how much you are forced to take out, a problem that could have likely been avoided or mitigated if you prepared for it in advance.

One step further, if you plan on leaving an IRA to your children, they will be subject to the ten-year rule discussed during the section on the horseman of taxes. The distributions they may need to take to deplete the account in ten years could force them into higher Medicare Part B premium brackets. These are all reasons for why you need to be preparing for what Medicare is going to look like for you and your spouse well in advance of the time you plan to sign up for your benefit.

Something to keep in mind. If, prior to retirement, you had household income and a MAGI level that puts you in a high Medicare Part B premium bracket, but you will have a lower MAGI after you retire, you can file for an exception. For example, if when you were sixty-three, your MAGI was above $103,000 and pushed you into a higher Medicare Part B bracket, but when you retire at age sixty-five, your expected MAGI is to be below the threshold, you can file a "Medicare Income-Related Monthly Adjustment Amount–Life-Changing Event" form. If approved, you will not be charged the higher Medicare Part B premium amount. This also applies to Part D premiums. A work stoppage is just one exception listed on the form. There are eight listed on the form that may be approved.

Medicare Part B comes with an annual deductible of $240 before it starts to pay. After that, Part B will generally cover 80 percent of the cost of your doctor's visits and outpatient services. You want to ensure you aren't on the hook for the 20 percent it doesn't cover because if you happen to need a $100,000 surgery, that makes you responsible for $20,000, and that doesn't include any of the other costs that might come along with recovery.

That is where Medigap or Medicare Advantage Plans, or Part C, come in, but before you talk about Medigap and Medicare Advantage, let's cover Part D first.

Medicare Part D

Medicare Part D covers your prescription drugs. Instead of being administered by the federal government like Parts A and B, it is provided through a private insurance company. Part D plans come in all different shapes and sizes, so you want to be matched up with the one that makes sense for you based on the type of prescriptions you take. It isn't uncommon for spouses to have different Part D plans. Medicare is administered on an individual basis, so you are simply selecting the right plan for you.

Like Medicare Part B, Medicare Part D includes a premium. Your premium will be based on the plan you select, but also, like Medicare Part B, your Part D premiums can be affected by your income level. Aside from paying the premium required by the plan you select, you could potentially pay up to an additional $85.80 a month. See the chart on the next page.

This increase in premium will only last for as long as the elevated income lasts, so if you only have a spike for one year, your premium increase should only last for a year as well. All the examples we explored when we discussed Part B about how your premiums can increase based on certain situations—selling properties, recognizing large gains, RMDs, inheriting an IRA—apply to your Part D premiums as well. If you are married, they apply to your spouse, too.

Starting in 2025, the maximum out-of-pocket spending cap for prescription drugs under a Part D plan will be $2,000. After you have spent that much out of pocket, you're done paying Part D copays and coinsurance for the year.[141] The plan premium doesn't count towards your out-of-pocket expense, and you still have to pay the premium even after you've reached your maximum out-of-pocket limit.

Limiting out-of-pocket spending is a significant change from 2024. Previous plans were subject to what became known as the donut hole. For 2024, once you and your Part D plan had spent $5,030 on covered drugs, you'd be in a coverage gap. This is when you enter the donut hole. When in the donut hole, you must pay up to 25 percent out-of-pocket on covered medications. You left the donut hole once you spent $8,000 out-of-pocket on covered drugs. At that point, you would enter what is known as the catastrophic coverage phase, and you would no longer pay out-of-pocket for your drug costs.

Table H – Medicare Part D 2025 Premium Table[142]

Beneficiaries Who File Individual Tax Returns With Modified Adjusted Gross Income:	Beneficiaries Who File Joint Tax Returns With Modified Adjusted Gross Income:	Income-Related Monthly Adjustment Amount
Less than or equal to $106,000	Less than or equal to $212,000	$0.00
Greater than $106,000 and less than or equal to $133,000	Greater than $212,000 and less than or equal to $266,000	13.70
Greater than $133,000 and less than or equal to $167,000	Greater than $266,000 and less than or equal to $334,000	35.30
Greater than $167,000 and less than or equal to $200,000	Greater than $334,000 and less than or equal to $400,000	57.00
Greater than $200,000 and less than $500,000	Greater than $400,000 and less than $750,000	78.60
Greater than or equal to $500,000	Greater than or equal to $750,000	85.80

This change makes Part D coverage more affordable for those on Medicare, but unfortunately, it also makes the program more expensive as a whole. With nearly half of the federal budget already being spent on entitlement programs, it will likely expedite the need for the federal government to increase taxes in the future. There is no free lunch. The money has to come from somewhere.

Plan premiums plus potentially paying $2,000 out-of-pocket for prescription drugs is still a lot of money to spend each year. That is why it is important to shop for the Part D plan that makes the most sense for you. Keep in mind different Part D plans cover different drugs, so you need to ensure your drugs are covered. The last thing you want to have happen is to pay for an expensive drug out-of-pocket because it's not covered under your plan. Not only that, the money you spend on your out-of-coverage drug won't count towards your maximum out-of-pocket. The right Part D plan can reduce the likelihood that you will end up hitting the limit.

As with Part B, you want to be sure to sign up for Part D when you become eligible. If you don't, there is a lifetime penalty. Even if you aren't taking any prescription drugs when you qualify for Medicare, it's still important to sign up for a Part D plan. You might find a plan with a zero monthly premium or a very low monthly premium. In the end, if you do need prescription drugs in the future, it will likely be a lot less expensive than being locked into a lifetime penalty for signing up late. The penalty for signing up late is 1 percent per month. That's 12 percent a year, and it is for life.[143]

Medicare Part C

Like Medicare Part D, Medigap and Medicare Advantage Plans are administered by private insurance companies, and they are designed to help fill in the gaps that Medicare Parts A, B, and D don't cover. Remember, you don't want to be on the hook for the 20 percent of costs that Medicare Part B isn't going to cover. That can be extremely expensive.

Deciding whether or not to go with a Medigap plan (otherwise known as a Medicare Supplement Insurance plan) along with Parts A and B, or a Medicare Advantage Plan (sometimes referred to as Part C) is a big decision that can have significant consequences. Just like with all the other decisions we have discussed throughout this book, it is important to take the time to ensure that you are making the right decision for you.

To help you decide which plan makes the most sense for you, we will first explain how each option operates along with some of the advantages and disadvantages of each program. We'll start with Medigap plans first before discussing Medicare Advantage Plans.

Medigap Or Medicare Supplement Insurance Plans

Medigap plans, or Medicare Supplement Insurance plans, are two names for the same thing and are designed to do exactly what it sounds like. They help supplement or fill in the gaps that Medicare Parts A, B, and D don't cover. There are several Medigap plans to choose from, and they are identified by different letters of the alphabet. There are currently ten different options, but some of those options have been phased out, such as Plan C and F. If you are a new enrollee, you won't be able to sign up for those plans.

The current plans you can choose from are plans A, B, C, D, F, G, K, L, M, or N. Plan G also offers a high-deductible option. Each plan offers specific types of coverage, which you can see in Table I, so just like you want to choose the right Part D plan based on your needs, you want to be sure to pick the right supplement plan based on your needs. Remember, the right plan for you might not be the same as your spouse.

Table I – Medigap Plan Coverage[144]

Medigap Benefit	Plan A	Plan B	Plan C	Plan D	Plan F*	Plan G*	Plan K	Plan L	Plan M	Plan N
Part A Coinsurance And Hospital Costs Up To An Additional 365 Days After Medicare Benefits Are Used	✓	✓	✓	✓	✓	✓	✓	✓	✓	✓
Part B Coinsurance or Copayment	✓	✓	✓	✓	✓	✓	50%	75%	✓	✓***
Blood Benefit (First 3 Pints)	✓	✓	✓	✓	✓	✓	50%	75%	✓	✓
Part A Hospice Care Coinsurance or Copayment	✓	✓	✓	✓	✓	✓	50%	75%	✓	✓
Skilled Nursing Facility Care Coinsurance	X	X	✓	✓	✓	✓	50%	75%	✓	✓
Part A Deductible	X	✓	✓	✓	✓	✓	50%	75%	50%	✓
Part B Deductible	X	X	✓	X	✓	X	X	X	X	X
Part B Excess Charge	X	X	X	X	✓	✓	X	X	X	X
Foreign Travel Emergency (Up To Plan Limits)	X	X	80%	80%	80%	80%	X	X	80%	80%
Out-Of-Pocket Limit	N/A	N/A	N/A	N/A	N/A	N/A	$7,060 in 2024 ($7,330 in 2025)	$3,530 in 2024 ($3,610 in 2025)	N/A	N/A

You may have heard of the "Cadillac" Medigap Plan F,[145] which is no longer available for new enrollees. Fortunately,

Plan G offers almost the same coverage as Plan F. The only difference is that Plan G does not cover your annual Part B deductible. Since Plan G is the most commonly selected supplement plan today, we'll use that to explain the benefits provided by a Medicare Supplement plan.

After you've paid your Medicare Part B deductible ($257 for 2025 and adjusted annually for inflation), and as long as you pay the monthly premium, which is separate from your Part B premium, a Plan G Medicare Supplement Insurance plan is going to cover your Part A coinsurance, deductible, and daily cost rate, we discussed previously. It is also going to cover your Part B coinsurance or copayment, which is the 20 percent Medicare Part B doesn't cover. There are some other benefits, but those are the major ones. Essentially, once you pay the deductible and monthly premium, if it is covered under Medicare, you don't pay anything else. So if you need to visit the hospital, need a surgery, or need to visit your doctor, if it is covered under Medicare, you won't receive a bill.

That sounds nice, but how much is the monthly premium? The monthly premium you pay for your Medicare Supplement Insurance plan will depend on your age, service area, and the company you choose for your protection. On average, a Plan G supplement will cost on average $129.38 a month for a sixty-five-year-old and $215.37 a month for an eighty-five-year-old.[146]

Medicare Supplement Insurance plans are regulated at the federal and state levels and administered through private insurance companies. That means Plan G is the same for company A as it is for company B, so how do you decide which company to go with?

If you decide to select Plan G, you may be tempted to simply pick the insurance company with the lowest rate. That is certainly what some insurance agents will recommend, but there are several other factors I encourage families to take into consideration when choosing their supplement plan, such as:

- What is the financial rating of the company that you are selecting? The financial rating of a company helps determine its ability to pay claims. You want a financially reputable company.
- What is their process for determining rate increases? They might be the most inexpensive company now, but if they have a history of higher-than-average rate increases, they might not be inexpensive for long.
- How is their customer service? If you have to call to discuss a charge, you want a company that is responsive to your needs.
- Do they offer any discounts for other family members to sign up with them? Some companies will offer a discount if your spouse or another family member is signed up as well.

With a Plan G Medigap plan or Medicare Supplement Insurance plan, as long as you pay your deductible and monthly premium, the rest is essentially covered, assuming Medicare covers it in general. That's one of the benefits of a supplement plan.

Another benefit is that you are not subject to a specific network. You can go wherever Medicare is accepted. This is especially beneficial if you plan to travel. Depending on which plan you choose, there is some foreign travel coverage. Using Plan G as our example, Plan G covers 80 percent of medically necessary emergency care costs during international travel. There is a $250 deductible and a $50,000 lifetime limit, so there isn't much coverage.

Realistically, if you are going to travel internationally, you will want to purchase additional healthcare coverage for your trip. However, if you are traveling anywhere in the United States, you'll be covered as long as the facility you go to accepts Medicare, which shouldn't be an issue as most major organizations do. There's no need to be concerned about whether you are in-network or out-of-network. Medigap or Medicare Supplement Insurance plans aren't your only option for covering the gap that Medicare Parts A, B, and D neglect. This is where Medicare Advantage Plans come in.

Medicare Advantage Plans

If you've ever seen an ad on TV or otherwise that boasts very low or even zero monthly premiums as it relates to Medicare, you are probably looking at a Medicare Advantage Plan. Medicare Advantage, which is also known as Part C, replaces Parts A and B and may offer additional benefits such as dental, vision and hearing. It is issued by private insurance carriers approved by Medicare. Lower monthly premiums is often one of the biggest benefits of a Medicare Advantage Plan. Unlike a Medigap plan, where you have to pay a monthly premium month in and month out, you only pay for your Medicare Advantage Plan if you need to use it. To be clear, some Medicare Advantage Plans do require a monthly premium, but even if you do select one with a monthly premium, the amount is likely much lower than a Medigap plan.

However, if you do need care, there is going to be a cost. Also, unlike a Medigap plan, where once you've paid your

Part B deductible and monthly premium, there is likely to be no more out-of-pocket cost on your part, you are likely going to pay when you need care under a Medicare Advantage Plan.

For example, if you need a ride in an ambulance, there is likely to be a copay. I'm using the word "likely" when discussing Medigap plans and Medicare Advantage Plans because there are several options in each category, and they offer different benefits. The goal is to simply help you understand what you can "likely" expect. As we have repeated ad nauseam, before selecting a plan, making sure you do your due diligence or having someone help you with the due diligence is important.

With a Medicare Advantage Plan, if you require a hospital or skilled nursing facility stay, you are likely going to be responsible for paying a per-day amount. You may be responsible for copays or coinsurance payments when visiting a doctor, receiving emergency care, or needing the use of medical equipment—the list goes on. The benefit of a Medicare Advantage Plan is you will only have to make these payments if you require them. Instead of making monthly payments like a Medigap plan, you pay for what you need. The downside is if you do need care, it can get expensive quickly.

There is a cap or a maximum out-of-pocket (MOOP) for the year. Your maximum out-of-pocket limit is the amount of money you will be required to pay for covered healthcare services in a plan year. If you hit your MOOP, your health plan will pay 100 percent of all covered healthcare costs for the rest of the year. The MOOP allowed for 2025 is $9,350 for a Medicare Advantage Plan. The plans can set lower limits.

Another thing to consider when deciding to choose a Medicare Advantage Plan is you will be subject to a network.

If you go out of network, as my grandfather did in the story at the beginning of this chapter, there will likely be an additional cost and potentially no coverage at all. That means you would be responsible for 100 percent of the cost of the care. Depending on what type of network you choose, if your doctor determines that you need to see a doctor or specialist outside of your network, it will take a referral, and it is up to the insurance company to decide whether it will approve it or not. There are other situations in which the insurance company can deny coverage as well.[147]

Medicare Advantage Plans will often include your Part D coverage as a single package. These are known as Medicare Advantage Prescription Drug Plans or MAPDs. Instead of having to shop for a Medigap plan and a prescription drug plan separately, MAPD plans allow you to have one plan that includes both aspects.

There are some unique perks or coverage options that come with certain Medicare Advantage Plans, such as fitness programs, gym memberships and discounts, and some vision, hearing, and dental services that are not going to be part of a Medigap plan. This is also something to consider when deciding on what type of coverage to choose.

A Medicare Advantage Plan can absolutely be the right type of plan for the right type of person. Considering your family history and belief you will likely stay relatively healthy throughout your retirement, a Medicare Advantage Plan may be the most cost-effective option for you. The downside is that it only takes a few years in a row to hit your MOOP and make you wish you had gone the Medigap route. Certainly, if you are someone who plans to travel within the United

States regularly throughout your retirement, it is possible that Medigap coverage makes the most sense. If you start with either a Medigap plan or a Medicare Advantage Plan, you may have the opportunity to switch, but that isn't always easy. We will address changing plans next.

Changing Plans

When you are first eligible for Medicare, this is called your initial enrollment period (IEP). If you don't currently have qualifying healthcare coverage (such as through an employer) when you turn age sixty-five, or you will lose qualifying coverage when you turn age sixty-five, your enrollment period starts three months before the month you turn sixty-five, includes the month you turn sixty-five, and ends three months after the month you turn sixty-five. During this seven-month period, you are considered guaranteed eligible despite any preexisting condition. No insurance company can turn you away. You can sign up for any Medigap or Medicare Advantage Plan you would like. This makes your IEP extremely important.

You do have the ability to change plans in the future, but after your IEP, insurance companies reserve the right to deny you coverage. Your current insurance company has to keep you, but a new insurance company doesn't have to take you. If you decide you want to change insurance companies or plans in the future, you will have to go through an underwriting process. This is where an insurance company will evaluate whether or not they want to take on the risk of insuring you based on your current and previous health conditions.

If you sign up for a Medigap plan, you can switch to another Medigap plan anytime throughout the year. This doesn't necessarily mean switching from Plan G to Plan N.

You could be keeping Plan G but switching from Plan G with company A to Plan G with company B. Your reason for doing this might be that company A had an abnormally high rate increase because the population they insure had a bad year from a health perspective. Now, company B has better rates, and, as we already discussed, Plan G with company B is going to cover everything Plan G covered with company A. Of course, you'll want to ensure company B is a reputable company and checks the other boxes we discussed as well.

In general, it is often good to shop your Medicap plan every couple of years, because different insurance companies do have different rate increases, so ensure you are getting the best rate and coverage for you.

Keep in mind that your ability to switch will be based on your ability to be accepted by company B after you go through underwriting. No insurance company is going to expect you to have perfect health, but some things can happen in your life that can prevent you from being able to switch to a new company. Those things might be related to heart issues, cancers, renal failure, the type of medications you might be taking, and other factors, so if you do switch, you always want to ensure you are switching to a company that you will be comfortable with for the long haul if it comes down to it. Unfortunately, health can turn for the worse quickly sometimes.

As stated, you can choose to change companies or plans anytime you want with a Medigap plan, but after your IEP, if you want to switch from a Medigap Plan to a Medicare Advantage Plan, you will have to wait for the annual Open Enrollment Period (OEP), which is from October 15 through December 7 each year.

If you are under a Medicare Advantage Plan, you can switch to a Medigap plan during the OEP as well. This is also the time you can change your Medicare Part D prescription drug plan if it makes sense to do so. Just like shopping for your Medigap plan, it is good to shop your prescription drug plan every so often because rates change, drug coverage changes, and the types of medications you take change.

If you want to switch from a Medicare Advantage Plan to another Medicare Advantage Plan, you will need to wait for the Medicare Advantage Open Enrollment Period (MA OEP), which is January 1–March 31 each year. During this time, you can also switch from a Medicare Advantage Plan to a Medigap plan and add a prescription drug plan if needed. If you are on a Medicare Advantage Plan and you like it, it is still good to shop the plan every year or so. Again, coverages change, rates change, and other perks change as well.

One thing to note: If you originally signed up for a Medigap plan, you can switch to a Medicare Advantage Plan during the OEP without going through underwriting. You are guaranteed eligible. You are allowed to do this one time, and it can even be on a trial basis. This is known as the Medicare Advantage trial rights.[148] If you are dissatisfied with the plan before the year is over, you can switch back to a Medigap plan without medical underwriting. After the year is up, if you want to return to a Medigap plan, you will be subject to underwriting and can be denied coverage. If you do switch back to a Medigap plan, you must go back to the same plan with the same insurance company, assuming it is still available.

If you originally signed up for a Medicare Advantage Plan during your IEP, if it has been less than a year and you have decided that you would rather have a Medigap plan as opposed to a Medicare Advantage Plan, you can also switch to a Medigap plan. These are nice nuances to be aware of.

The last Medicare period we will discuss is the Special Enrollment Period (SEP). If you lose your existing coverage, move outside of your service area, your Medicare plan changed, or your eligibility changed, this can open up a special window for you to change your coverage. For example, let's say you are part of a Medicare plan that you absolutely hate. If you move outside of your coverage area, you could regain your guaranteed eligibility rights and sign up for a new Medigap or Medicare Advantage Plan that you do want. Generally, if you are subject to a SEP, the period you have to sign up for a new plan is two to three months, depending on the qualifying event.

Medigap Plan Versus Medicare Advantage Plan

My parents and grandparents made choices based on their preferences and situations. Which plan you choose to go with and what subplan you choose is an individual choice. Spouses may end up on two different plans due to their individual needs and concerns. Due to having low or zero monthly premiums and only needing to pay when the plan is used, Medicare Advantage Plans have exploded in popularity. In 2008, only 22 percent of Medicare enrollees were in Advantage plans. Now, more than half of Medicare's sixty million Part A and Part B beneficiaries have opted for a Medicare Advantage Plan.[149] However, many Medicare beneficiaries still prefer the freedom and flexibility that Original Medicare provides through Medigap and Medicare Supplement Insurance plans, where they aren't confined to a network and are free to pick and choose what doctors they utilize.

If you can afford the monthly premiums, a Medigap plan appears to be the more conservative approach, especially given the fact that you will tend to spend more on healthcare the older you get, and by that time, switching is less feasible due to medical underwriting requirements.

As the popularity of Medicare Advantage programs has grown and insurance companies have gained more control over what is and isn't approved and what they are willing to pay hospitals and physicians for services, some problems have started to arise. Some hospitals have just outright dropped the acceptance of Medicare Advantage Plans,[150] and rural areas are potentially affected more as there are fewer options for care.[151] The options your network provides are something to consider when choosing a Medicare Advantage Plan. If you do choose a Medicare Advantage Plan, travel insurance is likely going to be a must. Being faced with an out-of-network expense can cause significant financial hardship.

Chapter Fourteen

HEALTH SAVINGS ACCOUNT

W hat if I told you there was an account available to you that allowed you to take a tax deduction for the money you placed in it, the money grew tax-free, and when you took the money out for qualifying medical expenses, you received it tax-free? You received a tax benefit on both ends, not just one. If you were paying attention to the section on the horseman of taxes, you already know what type of account this is. It is a health savings account, or HSA. Please note that to contribute to an HSA, you must be covered under a high-deductible health plan. Typically, your health plan will let you know if it is HSA eligible or not.

Normally, HSA funds can't be used to pay premiums for health insurance, but when you are on Medicare, the rules change. HSA funds can be used tax-free to pay for your Medicare premiums. Because of this, taking an HSA into retirement could be a significant advantage, but there are some rules you need to be aware of.

First, if you are turning age sixty-five, have already started drawing Social Security, and are contributing to an HSA, you need to stop your contributions the month prior to turning sixty-five. The reason for this is since you are already taking Social Security, you are automatically going to be enrolled in Medicare Part A. Once you are on Medicare, you can no longer make HSA contributions. If you don't stop in time or continue to contribute, there is an excise penalty.

Now, let's say you are turning sixty-five, you are contributing to an HSA, and you have not started drawing Social Security. You intend to continue to work until you are sixty-seven, and you have qualifying coverage through your employer. You can still contribute to the HSA. Since you haven't started drawing Social Security, you won't be automatically enrolled in Medicare Part A. However, before you retire at age sixty-seven, you will want to stop your HSA contributions six months before starting Medicare. This is because if you retire after the age of sixty-five, Medicare provides retroactive coverage for six months. In our example, if you retire at sixty-seven and sign up for Medicare, due to Medicare's retroactive coverage, your Medicare coverage actually started at age sixty-six and a half, and you can't contribute to an HSA and be on Medicare at the same time.

Before you think you can sneak in all your contributions prior to all this, Medicare has a rule for that, too. You can only contribute the pro-rata contribution amount for the year based on the number of months you were eligible to contribute to your HSA.

Lastly, when it comes to HSAs, you need to be careful about beneficiaries. Funds that are in an HSA can be passed to a spouse without issue. The spouse just assumes the HSA as their own, and the benefits continue. However, if you leave an HSA to a non-spouse beneficiary, you have some tax issues. Well, your beneficiary does, and here comes the horseman of taxes again, ready to claim his share.

When a non-spouse beneficiary inherits an HSA, a child, for example, the funds inside the account must be withdrawn and are subject to ordinary income tax in the year they are inherited. Ouch. HSA funds may be great for you and your spouse, but it is an account you want to ensure you fully utilize during your lifetime.

For more information and to access videos of explaining these important nuances about HSAs, please visit thefourhorsemenbook.com.

Medicare and how you are going to pay for it isn't the only thing you need to be concerned about when it comes to planning for how you mitigate the horseman of healthcare. You also need to be concerned about long-term care and your potential need for long-term care services in the future.

Chapter Fifteen

LONG-TERM CARE

Everyone thinks it isn't going to happen to them, but the reality is that an estimated 70 percent of those turning age sixty-five today are expected to need some form of long-term care service in their lifetime.[152] That doesn't necessarily mean full-blown confinement-based nursing home care. It can be as simple as needing someone to come to your house a few times a week to ensure you have everything you need. However, even the most basic form of long-term care service can be expensive. It's important to have a plan for how you are going to handle that expense if the need for it arises.

The different types of long-term care services are vast. Long-term care can include in-home care options. This type of care can be nonmedical, like assistance with cooking, cleaning, and running errands. It can also include help with bathing, dressing, and eating.

There are also social and support services provided in a community setting. Participants can join in planned activities with caregivers looking after them. Some programs also include personal care, transportation, medical management, and meals. This might be appropriate for someone who has a family member actively helping them, but needs help while that family member is at work.

Then, there are live-in facility options, from assisted living to nursing home care. An assisted living facility may include personal care and health services provided in a residential facility. The level of care is tailored to the resident's individual needs but isn't as extensive as nursing home care. People may consider assisted living when they don't need care around the clock, but they are also either unable or uncomfortable living independently in their own homes.

Lastly, we come to nursing home care, the type of care most people associate with long-term care services. This is confinement care. This is when nursing homes and residential facilities provide high levels of supervision and around-the-clock care.

How much can these services cost? In 2025, estimated costs for in-home nonmedical care can cost up to $6,068 a month on average ($72,816 per year), while a semiprivate room in a nursing home facility can cost up to $9,197 a month on average ($110,364 per year). Historically, the rising cost of long-term care services has outpaced the cost of general inflation,[153] and the problem doesn't appear to be getting any better. There are more people retiring today than at any other point in our nation's history, plus we are living longer than previous generations.

This creates a simple supply and demand issue. The cost of care is likely to increase as demand increases, and the supply of places that are able to provide the care needed remains limited. In 2045, when those turning age sixty-five today will be turning age eighty-four, homemaker services are estimated to cost up to $10,960 a month ($131,520 a year), and a semi-private room as a nursing home facility could cost up to $16,611 a month ($199,332 a year).[154]

Earlier, I wrote that ignoring your future tax liability in retirement is like going on a long road trip and ignoring the check engine light. You might be OK for a while, but eventually, you're likely going to run headfirst into some problems. Ignoring your future healthcare expenses, especially as they relate to long-term care services, is like embarking on a long trip and ignoring the fact that smoke is billowing from your engine as you pull out of the driveway. You better have a plan.

How To Pay For Long-Term Care

For a select few, the cost of paying out of pocket for a long-term care need, even if it is full-blown nursing home care, is no big deal, but most families can't afford to pay roughly $9,000 a month for care for very long without rapidly spending through their assets or leaving a surviving spouse financially destitute. Fortunately, there are several ways you can pay for long-term care needs.

Traditional Long-Term Care Policy

One of the more traditional ways to pay for long-term care is by purchasing a long-term care policy. This is where you pay a premium for a benefit you can use in the future to offset or pay for the cost of a long-term care service. These types of policies come in all different shapes and sizes and with varying benefits.

You could buy one of these policies with a one-time payment, but most people who purchase a long-term care policy pay for it by either making annual, semiannual, quarterly, or monthly payments. These policies, which can be very beneficial if you need care, have fallen out of favor for several reasons, and most insurance companies have stopped selling them altogether. If you have already purchased a long-term care policy, you may already have experience with the downsides.

One downside is cost. Premium payments are typically expensive to purchase for a benefit that is worth having. They are outside the budget for many families, and for those who can pay the premium, there are often better options.

Premium increases are another issue. With the cost of care increasing, many insurance companies are forced to raise rates. If a policyholder experiences a premium increase, they are forced to decide whether they are going to pay the additional premium or reduce the amount of coverage their policy provides. Neither is a great option.

What if you are fortunate enough to never need care? Most policies don't offer any return of premium. If you pass peacefully in your sleep and you never see a benefit from the policy, many families feel uncomfortable with that deal.

Lastly, like most insurance coverage, long-term care policies are very specific on what they will and will not pay for. If you want to receive care at home, a long-term care policy may not cover those expenditures. They are likely only going to pay if you need full-blown nursing home care. In other words, the most meaningful coverage is for the least pleasant outcomes.

While it is true that there is an estimated 70 percent chance you will need some form of long-term care service throughout your retirement, only 15 percent of those turning 65 are expected to spend more than two years in a nursing home,[155] so the majority of families really need coverage for the lower levels of care we discussed previously.

Medicaid Spend Down

Another way to cover the cost of a long-term care need, specifically nursing home care, is through a Medicaid spend down strategy. (Be sure not to confuse Medicare with Medicaid. Medicaid is a welfare program that provides health coverage for eligible low-income families. Medicare has very limited benefits when it comes to long-term care expenses, and generally only lasts up to one hundred days.) In this scenario, you either decided not to purchase any type of long-term care protection, or what you did purchase isn't enough to fully cover the cost of care for the projected length of stay in a nursing care facility. This means that you are going to be responsible for paying for the cost of care. This is where the Medicaid spend down strategy is often utilized.

Medicaid spend down is a type of estate planning strategy that strives to help a family protect as much of their assets as possible from long-term care expenses. Since it is a type of estate planning strategy, it typically requires the help of an attorney, with coordination from your financial advisor, to implement it correctly. Medicaid is regulated at the state level, which means the rules are going to vary from state to state. There are some commonalities, but you will want to work with an attorney in your area to ensure that you are implementing the right plan based on your state's regulations.

Medicaid is a type of welfare program for low-income families. If you are reading this book, you probably don't qualify as a low-income family. The goal of the Medicaid spend down strategy is to protect as much of a family's wealth and resources as possible by strategically reducing a family's assets through certain investment decisions, gifting, and other avenues to the point where Medicaid will take over paying for the cost of care.

Since Medicaid is regulated at the state level, it's impossible to provide a specific example based on the rules of each individual state. For that reason, the examples that I am going to provide are fairly generic but should still provide some insights into how a Medicaid spend down strategy is likely to work. God forbid you ever find yourself in that situation. We'll start with a married couple.

Suppose we have a married couple named David and Martha. Unfortunately, David needs to be placed into a nursing home, which is going to cost them $8,641 a month or $103,692 a year. David and Martha sacrificed and saved well for retirement, and they have been good stewards of their money throughout retirement, so much so that they have $1,500,000 in assets among their IRAs and their brokerage and savings accounts. Even with this being the case, the cost of $103,692 a year isn't sustainable for them for very long. Too long, and Martha could be left financially destitute.

For Medicaid to start paying for David's care, they are only allowed to have assets up to $154,140 for 2024 across all accounts. This is known as the community spouse resource allowance.[156] This is adjusted for inflation.

Since David needs care, they now have a choice to make. More specifically, Martha has a choice to make. Option (a): she can do nothing and continue to pay for David's care from their accounts until she reaches the community spouse resource allowance. At that point, Medicaid will start to pay for David's care. Option (b): Martha can choose to implement a Medicaid spend down strategy to protect as much of their assets as possible by reducing their assets through other means. Martha decides to go with option (b).

What can't Martha do? She can't simply gift $1,345,860 to her children in order to get down to the community spouse resource allowance. This is because Medicaid has something called the look-back rule. The look-back rule usually covers five years and is meant to prevent Medicaid applicants from inappropriately removing assets from the estate (i.e., gifting) to meet the community spouse resource allowance limit. Currently, only two states, California and New York, have a look-back period of less than five years. If assets are deemed to be inappropriately removed within the look-back period, a penalty will be assessed where the applicant will not qualify for Medicaid for a period of time.

For our example, let's say David applies for care on January 1, 2024, and lives in a state with a five-year look-back period. The look-back period would extend back to December 31, 2018. All financial transactions between these dates are subject to Medicaid review. The withdrawal of assets of any kind done prior to the five-year look-back period that is no longer included as part of David and Martha's estate will not be counted. Normal cost-of-living expenses aren't likely to violate Medicaid's look-back rule. The point of the rule is to identify transactions that could be construed as having the direct intent of reducing the value of one's assets. Even simple transactions you might not have even considered could be considered a violation. Examples could include:

- Gifting money to a grandchild for their birthday
- Transferring the title of a property to a family member for less than the fair market value
- Donating a vehicle to charity[157]

Because of the look-back period, the length of potential stay needs to be considered before implementing a Medicaid spend down strategy. According to a study found in the *Journal of the American Geriatrics Society*, of 1,817 nursing home residents who died while at the facility, the average length of stay was five months.[158]

If David's prognosis is that he will pass within the five-year look-back window, there may not be much that Martha can do other than pay for the care David needs from their assets. But what if the prognosis is different? In David's case, he's as healthy as an ox physically, but unfortunately, he has severe dementia. His stay could be upwards of ten years. If Martha wants to protect as much of the assets as possible, she needs to take action. Here's what that might look like.

For a married couple, if one spouse needs care and the other one doesn't, the primary residence is considered a protected asset along with one vehicle and certain other assets. This means that these assets don't count against the community spouse resource allowance. If there is still a mortgage on the house, Martha could use their assets to pay off the mortgage. Since the house is a protected asset, this does not count as a violation of the five-year rule. If there are repairs or improvements Martha wants to make to the house, she can do that as well. She could spend money on a new roof, paving the driveway, or remodeling the bathroom. By doing this, she is potentially increasing the value of the home if she does need to sell it in the future to recoup some funds. She could also sell the house and purchase a larger home if she wanted. None of these is a violation of the look-back rule, but there are limits to be aware of.

If she has an automobile loan, she can pay that off. She can sell her vehicle and purchase a new vehicle. One vehicle is considered a protected asset, so this would not be in violation of the look-back rule.

Martha could set up an irrevocable funeral expense trust to pay for funeral and burial costs for her and David upon their passing. There are state-specific limitations to this, but this is another way to turn countable assets under Medicaid into noncountable assets.

Martha has other options, but it is likely that even after exhausting all the options that make sense for her, she will still be above the community spouse resource allowance. This is when gifting comes in.

Let's say after exhausting the previous options, the assets are still around $1,250,000. Martha needs to get down to $154,140. She still has $1,095,860 to go. She will need to keep enough money to pay for David's care for five years to cover the look-back period. Considering the increasing cost of care and taxes owed on the withdrawals, we could roughly estimate that she will need $650,000 to cover the cost of David's care for five years. That means Martha still needs to reduce their assets by $445,860 (community spouse resource allowance of $154,140 + cost needed for care of $650,000 = $804,140 projected allowable and required assets) (total unprotected assets of $1,250,000 - $804,140 projected allowable and required assets = $445,860 reduction needed). This is where gifting comes into play.

Depending on the type of account the money comes from, taxes are going to have to be paid on withdrawals. That includes withdrawals made to pay for David's care, withdrawals made to turn counted assets into uncounted assets, and withdrawals made to make gifts. Unfortunately, sometimes, a family finds themselves in a position where there is no good option. Go with the option that does the least damage.

Martha decides to withdraw the $445,860, pay the tax, and gift it to their daughter for safekeeping. Trust is a big factor in this strategy. Once you make a gift, the money is no longer yours. That is the point of the gift: to get the assets out of your name. Martha trusts her daughter and informs her to keep the money safe, as she will likely need it to help support her in the future.

After the five-year look-back period is over, Martha has covered the cost of David's care, and she only has the community spouse resource allowance left; Medicaid will cover the cost of David's care from that point forward. There is a lot that goes into this strategy, and this is the most basic of examples, which is why it is important to work with an attorney and financial advisor who can help you make the right decision and implement that right strategy based on your situation and your state-specific rules.

If you are single and need long-term care but lack coverage, there are two options. Option (a) is to use current assets to pay for your care for as long as you can until you only have $2,000 in assets left. That is the asset limit in most states for a single individual. Once this happens, Medicaid will start paying for your care. There are still some strategies to turn countable assets into non-countable assets, but since there is no spouse, none of the assets, like a house, vehicle, or retirement assets, are considered exempt. They must be used to pay for your care.

Option (b) is a Medicare spend down strategy. This can still be utilized to protect as many assets as possible. If the prognosis is that care will last longer than five years (or whatever the look-back period is for the state of residence), those years of the cost of care will need to be retained to pay for the care during the look-back period. The rest of the assets can be gifted so that when the look-back period is over, the resource limit will be achieved, and Medicaid will start to pay for the cost of care.

Important Notes On Medicaid Spend Down

Gifting

To protect themselves against a Medicaid spend down situation, some families start to make strategic decisions to reduce the amount of their assets earlier in retirement. This comes with advantages and disadvantages.

One common strategy is gifting. Some families will decide to start gifting money, mainly to other family members such as children or grandchildren, well before they anticipate having a long-term care need. If you have excess wealth, this can be a great strategy, especially if you want to see others enjoy the money while you are alive. I'll often refer to it as a living legacy when talking with families, but you should use caution when implementing this strategy.

When you gift money, take into consideration the potential compound interest that you are gifting away. Again, I'll reference the words often attributed to Albert Einstein, "Compound interest is the eighth wonder of the world. He who understands it, earns it. He who doesn't, pays it." So, if you gift $25,000 when you are seventy years old, you shouldn't think of it as $25,000. Think of it as $50,000 or even $75,000 because that is the potential of what that money could turn into over your remaining life expectancy were it to stay invested. When you make a gift, you are also giving away the future growth of that money.

That isn't to say that gifting can't be a great strategy. It can be. Another option might be to gift that money to a specific type of trust where growth can still occur, but it will no longer be included as a countable asset in a Medicaid spend down situation. We'll discuss more about that in chapter 17 when we talk about the legal documents you should consider having.

Another type of gifting strategy is transferring the title of a home or property. Typically, this is also done with children. Let's say you have a piece of property that has been in the family for years. Whether you are married or not, it isn't a protected asset, because it isn't the primary residence. You're concerned about the potential that the property would need to be sold in the event of a long-term care expense, so you decide to gift the property to your three children. The advantage is that if you gift the property five years (or the applicable look-back period) prior to having a long-term care need, it will be outside the scope of the look-back period for Medicaid. The downside is that when you gifted the property, you also gifted your cost basis.

What is the cost basis? The cost basis is the original valuation of an asset for tax purposes. Let's assume that you purchased the property twenty years ago for $100,000. Because of the growth of real estate prices in the surrounding area, the property is now worth $250,000. If your children inherit the property after you pass, they will receive a step-up in cost basis to $250,000. If they sell the property for $250,000, then they will owe no tax because of the step-up in basis. But if you gift the property, you also gift your cost basis. In our example, your cost basis is $100,000. If your children sell the property for $250,000 now, they will have a capital gain of $150,000, the difference between the basis and the amount the property was sold for.

The same is true if you give stock or another type of appreciated asset (an asset that has increased in value). Maybe in our scenario, you aren't concerned about them not getting the step up because the purpose is for them to keep the property, but as already indicated, the gifting of cost basis applies to other gifts as well.

Beneficiaries

Checking beneficiaries is an important step when going through Medicaid spend down. Let's go back to our example of David and Martha. Originally, when David and Martha designated who they wanted to be as their beneficiaries on their accounts, they made each other the primary beneficiary on all their accounts. This is usually standard practice for a married couple unless it is a second marriage or there are other estate-planning strategies being implemented.

Once David needs care, Martha needs to update her beneficiary designations. If David passes and all his assets go to

Martha, that's not a problem. Martha isn't the one who needs care. If Martha passes, and David remains the beneficiary of her accounts, now there's a problem. Whatever funds David receives as a beneficiary are not likely to be considered as noncountable assets for Medicaid. Therefore, those funds are going to have to be used for his care. If Martha passes, he will no longer be married, and the community spouse resource allowance no longer applies. This puts even more of the assets at risk. If Martha wants to protect the assets from Medicaid spend down in the event something happens to her while David needs care, she should remove David as her beneficiary. For many, this means moving their children to the primary beneficiary position. Martha could also set up a trust or other entity to be her primary beneficiary.

If David has any family members who have him listed as a beneficiary of an asset, they likely want to change the beneficiary designation if they are able. Just like in the previous situation we discussed with Martha, if David inherits an asset, it will likely have to be used in some capacity for his care.

Medicaid Estate Recovery Program

Just because there were assets considered noncountable for Medicaid while care was needed and the recipient was alive does not mean that the assets will still be safe if the recipient passes. For this, we will once again go back to our example of David and Martha. For David and Martha, the house is a protected asset that is not subject to the Medicaid spend down strategy. This is because they are married, David is the one who needs care, and Martha is living in the home. The primary residence is protected, but Martha isn't out of the woods yet. That is because of something called the Medicaid

Estate Recovery Program (MERP). MERP is a program that seeks reimbursement of all long-term care costs that are paid for by a Medicaid beneficiary by Medicaid.[159,160]

When David passes, Martha will be free to live in the home for as long as she is able or until she passes. In this example, once Martha has passed, MERP will kick in. A letter will be sent to Martha's estate asking for reimbursement of the funds used by Medicaid to provide for David's care. If Medicaid paid $250,000 for David's care, that is the amount they will seek to receive from Martha's estate. This is when previously noncountable assets, like a primary residence, are no longer protected.

In most states, MERP is only applied to assets going through probate. Since most investment accounts are going to include a named beneficiary and thus avoid probate, those aren't a concern, but a house could be, which is why we are using it for this example. If Martha doesn't take the appropriate steps to protect the home from MERP upon her passing, her children could be forced to sell the home and use the funds for Medicaid reimbursement. There are exceptions for when MERP applies and doesn't apply, and there are ways to prevent assets from being subject to MERP entirely. This is just another example of why working with the right qualified professionals through a spend down situation is so important.

There are so many things to be aware of when going through a Medicaid spend down situation. It's too big of a topic to try and cover all the details in this book, and it is impossible to list all the nuances that exist in every state. For example, what if David is part owner of a property or business with other individuals? His share of that asset counts toward his asset limit.

What are his options in this scenario? Will he need to divest from his ownership? These are all questions that are going to take the help and insight of an attorney, tax professional, and competent financial advisor, so be sure to get the advice you need if ever you find you might be in this situation.

Life Insurance To Help Offset Long-Term Care Expenses

One strategy that is rapidly increasing in popularity as a way to help offset the cost of a long-term care need is through the use of a life insurance policy. This strategy isn't appropriate for everyone, but it does have some advantages.

In this situation, we are discussing a permanent life insurance policy not a term insurance policy. A term insurance policy is life insurance that provides a specified amount of coverage at a fixed rate for a specified period. The benefit of a term insurance policy is it typically gives you coverage (death benefit) for the least amount of dollars. This is typically suitable for someone who needs coverage based on a specific set of circumstances for the period or term. For example, a younger person might purchase a thirty-year term policy to protect the family against an early demise while there are young children still at home, a mortgage, and not much saved for retirement. By the end of the thirty-year term, the children will likely be out on their own, the house will be paid off or close to paid off, and there should be more saved for retirement, so the need for life insurance in the traditional sense often diminishes.

The downside of the term insurance policy is that once the term is up, the life insurance goes away. You won't receive any of your premium payments back, but your family will be thankful for the protection if anything were to happen to you during the term.

A permanent policy is one that is generally projected to remain in effect throughout your lifetime, as long as sufficient premiums are paid. Under this scenario, in some cases, you make a single premium payment, but more likely, you will make premium payments over a specific period of time—five, seven, and ten years are common payment periods—or you make premium payments up until death. As with all life insurance policies, you are using the premium payments you are putting in to leverage those dollars for a higher death benefit than the premiums you paid.

To help offset the cost of long-term care and provide a more attractive solution than traditional long-term care insurance policies, many insurance companies have begun to include an accelerated death-benefit option in their permanent policies, some of which may require an additional annual fee but not all. This allows you to access the death benefit of the policy early if you have a long-term care need, and since you are accessing the death benefit, you get to receive the funds tax-free.

In order to qualify for the accelerated benefit, you will have to have a doctor sign off stating that you are unable to perform at least two of the six activities of daily living. These include:

- Bathing
- Dressing
- Toileting
- Transferring
- Eating
- Continence

If you are unable to perform two of these functions, you can access funds from the death benefit of your policy early to help pay for the care you need. Accelerated death benefits come in all different shapes and sizes, so you will want to know exactly how your policy is designed to work. One of the biggest benefits of the accelerated benefit over a traditional long-term care policy is your ability to use the funds. Once you qualify, you can access the funds. There is no stipulation on how the funds must be used. This provides you with freedom and flexibility that traditional long-term care policies do not.

This is significant because you have the freedom to use the funds for homemaker services, community care services, or nursing home care. This is a significant benefit, considering that as many as 70 percent of those turning sixty-five today are expected to need some form of long-term care service, but only 5 percent will need nursing home care. On top of that, the 5 percent who do need nursing home care spend an average of less than two and a half years there.

There are costs to owning a permanent life insurance policy, as there are with most financial vehicles so you will want to weigh the cost against the benefit. What is particularly attractive about the life insurance strategy is someone you love is going to receive the money. If you are fortunate not to need long-term care during your lifetime, the death benefit of the life insurance policy will pass tax-free to your beneficiaries. If you do need care, it is there for you to use. Even if you need care and you don't utilize all the available death benefits, the portion that you didn't use will pass to your beneficiaries tax-free.[161]

If you choose to utilize a life insurance policy that also grows cash value like the one discussed in the section on the horseman of taxes, you can have a policy that grows cash value tax-free that you could use later in retirement for income, gain some long-term care protection, and secure a tax-free benefit to your beneficiaries. This type of strategy can also be used to help replace the income of a surviving spouse and protect against the horseman of longevity.

Depending on the type of policy you choose, this can also help fill a portion of the attribute of protection that was discussed in the section on the horseman of inflation. You can purchase a policy where the interest growth of your cash value is linked to the market with a cap, but you take on none of the downside risk of the market similar to a fixed indexed annuity.

Life insurance policies come in all different shapes and sizes, and typically require medical and financial underwriting to qualify. While the thought that one vehicle could help you combat all four horsemen at once is attractive, that doesn't mean it's possible or the right option. It can make sense for a portion of your overall plan, but there is no perfect investment vehicle.

Even with a traditional long-term-care or life insurance policy, a Medicare spend down strategy may need to be implemented for an extended long-term-care stay. This is because the benefit of any of those policies is going to run out eventually. The main benefit of these policies is that having them in place gives you the opportunity to protect more of your assets than you would if you had no protection at all.

Long-Term Care Conclusion

Whether you decide to go with a traditional long-term-care policy, a life insurance policy, or just plan to implement a Medicaid spend down strategy, you want to know what your plan is going to be before you end up in the situation where you need care, because as we discussed briefly, there are plenty of things you can be doing in advance to help protect your assets.

The one thing I would encourage you not to do is do nothing. Have a conversation with your spouse, your attorney, your tax professional, and your financial advisor, so you know what your plan is. While I don't disagree with hoping for the best, it is always good to plan ahead. We all want to believe it isn't going to happen to us, but we all probably know someone it has happened to. You have a greater chance of needing some form of long-term care service in your lifetime than not needing it. You should plan accordingly.

Chapter Sixteen

Health—
Beyond Investments

H ealth and wellness have always been a big part of my life. My mother is a nurse. My older sister is an emergency room doctor, and my wife is a nurse practitioner. The first time I was ever introduced to Fruit Loops was the first time I stayed overnight at a friend's house. My mom didn't allow that kind of stuff in the house while we were growing up. To this day, I still train regularly four to five days a week with weightlifting and running, and outside of the occasional cheat meal, I avoid added sugars like the plague.

I bring this up not to gloat but to tell you that mitigating the horseman of healthcare is much more than making sure you have the right financial plan and investment selection. How much you end up spending on healthcare in retirement, how well you live in retirement, and how long you live are likely to be greatly influenced by the cumulative decisions you choose to make day by day. It is imperative that you become the CEO of your own health. This is a topic I am extremely passionate about, and I would love to write a whole book on it one day. For now, I want to give you enough to convince you to take this seriously, because it really is life-and-death.

In his book *Life Force*, Tony Robbins describes the following scenario.[162] You're standing on a riverbank when suddenly you see someone drowning. Without a second thought, you jump in to save the person. You drag them to shore, revive them, and as soon as you do, there are two more people in the river drowning. You muster up all your strength, jump in, and rescue the other two people. You revive them, and as soon as you do, to your dismay, you see three more people drowning in the river. You rush in to save them, but there's a problem. You spend all your time saving people drowning in the river that you never have time to go upstream to find out who on earth is throwing all these helpless people in. You never get the opportunity to solve the root problem. Welcome to 99 percent of healthcare in America.

Most doctors are great people who decided to become doctors because they truly want to help people and make a positive impact on the world. Doctors get paid well, but it isn't about the money. Think about it. The cost of medical school is not only outrageously monetarily expensive but also grueling both physically and mentally. Plus, finishing medical school is only half the battle.

After that, you get average pay at best, working inhumane hours for several years in residency. Most people with that level of intelligence and commitment could find themselves making a lot more money doing something else. Once they become doctors, they quickly realize they are spending most, if not all, of their time pulling people from the river without ever having the opportunity to go upstream to see who is throwing the people in. They spend their time patching patients up as fast as they can, only to turn around and see several more people drowning. It's a grueling profession. It's no wonder that doctors are far more likely to die by suicide than the general population.[163]

In his book *Outlive*, Peter Attia, MD, describes our current healthcare situation as Medicine 2.0. Medicine 1.0 was figuring out the basics, like what part of the body is responsible for what function. Medicine 2.0 is where we learned about germs, which led to improved sanitary practices and the development of antibiotics. Basically, medicine 2.0 is defined as trying to fix things after you have found they're broken. Medicine 3.0, as Attia describes it, "is not to patch people up and get them out the door, removing their tumors and hoping for the best, but rather to prevent the tumors from appearing and spreading in the first place."[164]

You may have heard the saying that an ounce of prevention is worth a pound of cure. It happens to be true. In his book, Attia talks about a different set of horsemen. These four horsemen are heart disease, cancer, neurodegenerative disease, and type 2 diabetes and related metabolic dysfunction.[165] The overwhelming likelihood is that any one of us will die from one of these causes rather than any other. These diseases start to grow long before they are ever diagnosed. They develop over a long process, years, sometimes even decades, and are often a result of the compounding effect of our daily decisions. Certainly, environment, genetics, and other risk factors play a role, but one of the common themes throughout the book is that our individual choices play the biggest part.[166] To me, that's good news because anyone can choose to make different decisions.

If you want to get the most out of your life and the most out of your retirement, as I stated previously, you need to become the CEO of your own health. Despite their best efforts, doctors simply don't have the capacity to keep up with all new information and new discoveries. That isn't a knock on doctors. I love doctors. I'm glad I live in a world where doctors exist. I have doctors in my family, and if you are a doctor, please don't hear what I'm not saying. I'm not saying that you aren't good at what you do. You are probably very good at what you do, but unfortunately, our current system is not set up for prevention.

During a lecture at Harvard Medical School, Martín-J. Sepúlveda projected the half-life of medical knowledge would soon be seventy-three days. That means that half of the information and knowledge someone obtained during medical school will be outdated within seventy-three days.[167] That is how fast new information, new discoveries, and new knowledge is coming out. At that rate, how can anyone keep up? You have a much better opportunity to keep up on yourself than a doctor that has to keep up with you and hundreds of other patients. That is why I am encouraging you to do your own research and invest the time in educating yourself on how to exercise and eat better in addition to learning about new breakthroughs that are happening daily. Maybe you simply start with the two books mentioned in this section, and don't convince yourself that it is too late to start. If you are alive and breathing, it isn't too late.

My last point in this section is this. Retiring, completely leaving the workforce is a decision that many families don't take seriously enough. Retirement has somewhat become a reflex in our society, but like I mentioned in the very beginning of this book, it is a relatively new phenomenon.

Think about your work. For most families it makes up a large portion of their social network. It gives them meaning and purpose. It helps them feel fulfilled. On an anecdotal level, the happiest families that I observe are the ones that continue to work while being "retired." That doesn't mean that if you have a physically or mentally draining job you shouldn't retire. It simply means that completely retiring from the workforce isn't the best for some families, and it doesn't have anything to do with finances.

It all comes down to making sure you are retiring *to* something and not *from* something. Once you retire, how are you going to fill your time? What is your plan? How are you going to continue to derive meaning and purpose in your life? These are serious questions that need serious answers, and there is scientific evidence to support it. One study showed that nearly one in three retirees reported feelings of depression, a higher rate than the general population.[168] Various healthcare conditions and general life situations play into this, but many cite missing the structure of their job and the lack feeling like they are contributing to something greater than themselves.

All this is to say that your plan for retirement needs to include a plan for how you are going to spend your time. Many people find a part-time job that they enjoy or a place to volunteer and give back. Some socialize with friends and are deeply involved in the lives of their grandchildren. I know families that do group workouts, playing sports such as golf, tennis, fishing, pickleball, swimming, cycling, running, or softball.

Become the CEO of your own health and have a plan for how you are going to spend your time in retirement and continue to derive purpose in your life. That's a recipe for success.

The Horseman Of Healthcare

From choosing the right Medicare plan, having a plan for long-term care needs, and becoming the CEO of your own health, we've covered a lot of ground talking about the horseman of healthcare. There is a lot to ensure you get right.

This book is about helping you successfully mitigate the four horsemen of retirement, and it wouldn't be complete unless we talked about how you can do this once you have departed from this earth. No one wants to overcome the horsemen throughout their retirement only to allow them to wreak havoc on what they have worked so hard to accomplish after they're gone. For this, we move on to your legacy.

PART V

BEYOND THE FOUR HORSEMEN— LEGACY PLANNING

Chapter Seventeen

LEGACY PLANNING

Whether your intent is to leave a large inheritance, have the last check bounce, or somewhere in the middle, there are going to be assets left behind after you pass away, and there are three choices for where that money goes: your family/friends, charity, or the IRS. Whether you want to leave a large inheritance or not, most families would like to leave as little to the IRS as possible.

We'll start with the basics. Typically, there are four legal estate planning documents that estate planning attorneys suggest every family considers.

Basic Estate Planning Documents

Last Will And Testament

A last will and testament, commonly referred to simply as a will, is just a document with instructions to the probate court on how you want your assets to be divided after you're gone. Probate court is the part of the judicial system that oversees the handling of wills, estates, conservatorships, and guardianships.[169] When you create a will, you will not only describe how you want your assets to be dispersed, but you will also name an executor to oversee the process. It is the responsibility of the executor and the probate court to ensure that your final wishes are followed.

If you pass without a will, that is called dying intestate. This process is handled based on state law. Typically, your case will be brought to the probate court, and an administrator will be appointed to manage the affairs of your estate. Who becomes the administrator is dictated by state law, and some states have strict laws when it comes to who can be an administrator. For example, some states require the administrator to be a resident of the state of the deceased. This means that if you pass and there is no close relative in the state, someone completely unrelated to you could be appointed as the administrator of your estate. Your assets will be divided based on state law, which may or may not be conducive to your wishes.

Even with a will, an estate that is going through the probate process can be contested. We will discuss that in a moment, but there is a higher likelihood of an estate being contested if you die intestate without a will. This leads to expenses as the time your estate remains in probate lengthens and attorneys' fees escalate. The bottom line is to consider having a current will in place. Current means reviewing it every three to five years, and it is a good idea to work with a qualified attorney. You can do it yourself, but there are specific rules that must be followed to ensure the will is valid.

Durable Power Of Attorney

The second legal document you want to consider is a durable power of attorney. This allows someone to act in your best interest while you are alive if ever you're incapacitated or can no longer make decisions on your own. The durable part of the power of attorney means that it ends at death. Once you pass, your will takes over.

Here's a great example; we will assume another married couple, Joe and Nancy. Joe recently had an accident and is no longer able to make financial decisions on his own. Thankfully, Joe and Nancy had their legal documents prepared in advance, and Nancy has already been designated as Joe's durable power of attorney.

Nancy stayed home to help raise the children throughout the majority of her career and spent time volunteering at their church. Because of this, the bulk of their retirement assets were in an IRA in Joe's name. Nancy needs to take extra money from the IRA to help pay for Joe's care. For the financial institution to release funds to Nancy, a durable power of attorney is required. That's no problem since they took care of getting that in place in advance. Nancy can access the funds and continue to pay the bills associated with Joe's care without worry.

If no durable power of attorney was created ahead of time, a court would likely appoint a spouse as a power of attorney, but that isn't an overnight process. That is why it is better to have it done in advance. If you are single, you especially want to name your power of attorney.

When putting together your durable power of attorney, you have the ability to name a successor's power of attorney. This is a good idea. What if you are a married couple, and both of you experience an accident at the same time? What if your first choice of power of attorney decides the gig isn't for them, which they are allowed to do? It is always a good idea to have a successor power of attorney. Don't leave it up to the court to decide who will be it for you.

There's much more to the durable power of attorney, but the last thing I will mention here is that you want to ensure you reinstate it every three to five years. With most financial institutions, if you try to hand them a power of attorney that is ten years old, they may not accept it, because they can't confidently say that this is still the wish of the person who is incapacitated. Just like your will, it is good to review. It isn't a one-and-done type of thing.

Living Will

The third legal document you want to consider is a living will. This provides a directive on what you want to be done in those hard-and-fast moments if you are ever incapacitated. What types of measures do you want to be taken or not taken if you are ever in a medical situation where you are unable to make your own decisions? A living will provides those types of advance decisions to physicians and family members.

This is important for several reasons. Maybe there are certain procedures that you don't want to be taken because they are against your religious beliefs. Perhaps there are specific types of care that you only want to be implemented for a certain period. Lastly, a living will takes the pressure off the family. It helps remove the guilt aspect. Family members no longer have to guess and potentially fight about what you may or may not have wanted. You have already laid it out, and they can have the peace of mind of knowing that they are following your wishes.

This is what happened to my Uncle David. Unfortunately, at the age of fifty-eight, he suffered a series of strokes after a blood clot caused by untreated atrial fibrillation was launched into his brain and spread like a shotgun blast. As you can imagine, his family was devastated. Rather than having to guess as to what type of care he would have wanted, he had it all spelled out in his living will. He certainly didn't intend to die from a propulsion of blood clots to his brain at the age of fifty-eight. He did, however, get to go out the way he wanted if he ever found himself in that situation because he prepared in advance. At a minimum, his family could be confident in that. No guilt added to the already heart-wrenching experience.

Durable Power Of Attorney For Healthcare Decisions

The fourth legal document you want to consider is your durable power of attorney for healthcare decisions. Again, durable means it ends at death. Where the durable power of attorney we discussed previously deals largely with financial situations, a durable power of attorney for healthcare decisions does exactly what you might think it does. It appoints someone to act in your best interest to make healthcare decisions for you if you are ever incapacitated.

You might have a living will in place, but it is impossible to account in advance for all of life's contingencies. This is where your power of attorney for healthcare steps in. Just like the previous power of attorney document we discussed, it is a good idea to name a successor power of attorney. Also, be sure to review and reinstate your durable power of attorney for healthcare decisions document every three to five years.

Basic Estate Planning Documents Conclusion

This is simply brushing the surface when it comes to the basic estate planning documents, but they are something I encourage every family to take care of. Unfortunately, only about two out of every ten families I meet with for the first time have their legal documents taken care of, and often, even if they do have them taken care of, they are outdated. It is not something you want to put off. Everyone thinks they have plenty of time and they'll get to it later.

For the majority of families, getting these legal documents in place is a process with a quick turnaround of about two weeks. It's going to cost some money, but I encourage you to seek the help of an attorney licensed in your state. In most cases, you are looking at a range of $500 to $1,000, depending on your situation, and sometimes even less. It is a small price to pay compared to the potentially avoidable costs, legal fees, and family struggles that not having your basic legal documents can produce. Don't come all this way to overcome the horsemen just to get defeated by something that is so easy to take care of but has such a big impact.

Trusts

We briefly touched on some potential uses for trusts in our discussion on how to overcome the horseman of taxes. Trusts come in all different shapes and sizes, and there are lots of rules that dictate what you can and cannot do with certain trusts. At the risk of sounding like a broken record, be sure to work with an attorney, tax professional, and financial advisor who are familiar with the rules and have the ability to guide you to the best solutions for your situation.

As we saw in the section on the horseman of taxes, trusts can provide a unique way to reduce and potentially even eliminate taxes in some situations. That's a great thing in my opinion, and we only grazed the surface during that time. Trusts can also be a great way to help you achieve your other estate planning goals.

Maybe you have concerns about your estate being contested during the probate process, or you would prefer your assets not go through the public forum of the probate court. A trust can help you reduce how contestable your estate is and keep things more private.

It also gives you greater control from the grave. If you are worried about a child who can be a spendthrift, you can designate certain milestones that have to be achieved before the funds are released. Maybe you are part of a blended family or have had multiple marriages and want to be sure that the funds go the way you want. A trust can be a solution to that. A trust can help ensure that you don't accidentally disinherit someone. If you have a really large estate, using a trust can also ensure that you are maximizing your federal estate and gift tax exemption. This is where we start to get into the upper echelon of working to save millions of dollars in taxes.

There are many reasons for utilizing a trust, and they can help you overcome the horsemen in many ways. Ultimately, however, a trust is just a means to an end. If you can get to the end that you have in mind without using a trust, it is just as well. Oftentimes, ensuring you have the right beneficiary designations on your accounts is enough to suffice. Accounts with named beneficiaries also have the ability to completely bypass probate. If you need to use a trust, it is a great tool, but ensure you need one first.

Beneficiaries

Always take the time to ensure that you check your beneficiary designations. Children move, change last names, get divorced, have children of their own, and other life situations occur, which can all be reasons why you need to update your beneficiary information.

In many states, you can add beneficiary designations to your home, rental properties, land, and other related assets by adding a transfer-on-death designation, which adds beneficiaries to the property. This is a legal document that can be completed with the help of an attorney and filed with your local government. Now, instead of the asset passing through probate, it will pass directly to the named beneficiaries, cutting down the length of time the assets are received and the cost of the probate process.

Transfer on death designations can also be added to vehicles, boats, RVs, ATVs, and other titled assets. Most of the time, the local bureau of motor vehicles can assist with this process. Again, adding this designation allows the asset to avoid probate, reducing time and cost.

Payable on death designations should be added to bank accounts for the same reason. Then assets at the bank can quickly become accessible to the named beneficiaries to help take care of final expenses instead of having to come up with the money out of pocket with the hope of being reimbursed later.

We're talking about simple steps, but these are the types of details you don't want to miss in the quest to overcome the horsemen. You don't want to get all the big things right just to trip over something small.

Life Insurance

If you really want to maximize the value of your estate at death, provide quick liquidity to your beneficiaries, and leverage a tax-free death benefit, I suggest you consider life insurance. The purpose of all life insurance is to create leverage. You leverage existing dollars to create a larger sum in the future.

We've talked about the benefits of life insurance in several capacities already. It is a legacy tool for your estate and your loved ones and could also be used to fulfill a portion of what you need in the attribute of protection. It can be used as a tax-free source of income and to help offset future long-term care costs.

None of those benefits of life insurance are what most people think about when they think about life insurance. Most people think about life insurance in the traditional sense of leveraging smaller payments for a much larger payment in the future, often in the form of a tax-free death benefit. That is what we are discussing here now, and we touched on the concept of using life insurance in the estate planning process during the section on overcoming the horseman of taxes when we discussed Rick and Betty's situation. They were able to sell their medical building, completely eliminate the tax on the sale, create a tax deduction, and fund a life insurance policy that left over $4,000,000 tax-free to their two daughters.

The last step in that process that we didn't discuss is the concept of having life insurance held inside of an irrevocable life insurance trust (ILIT). By placing their life insurance policy inside of the ILIT, Rick and Betty eliminated the possibility of this asset being stripped away by a Medicaid spend down situation if one of them ended up needing care. Of course, the ILIT would need to be created and funded five years prior to needing care to avoid the look-back period, which they accomplished well in advance.

Life insurance, in combination with proper estate planning, can have a significant impact on how much you leave behind and how taxable it is. As we said at the beginning of this section, you don't want to do everything right to mitigate the horsemen, only to lose the battle after you are gone.

As a quick disclaimer, I would like to say we haven't dived into products too often in this book. That's because that really isn't the point. There are often several ways to reach a particular goal, but life insurance has come up several times because of its versatility. Realistically, most families opt not to purchase a life insurance policy as part of their retirement plan. It can be an effective tool for the families who benefit, but it isn't the right tool for everyone. There is no one-size-fits-all solution.

Legacy Planning Conclusion

Legacy planning is an essential part of mitigating the horsemen, and it is something that is built throughout the whole planning process. As we've seen, it often takes the coordination of multiple professionals to get it right. In some cases, this can be expensive, but expensive is a relative term. Expensive compared to what? That is what we will talk about next.

Fees

No one likes to overpay. We all want to feel like we are getting the value out of what we are paying for. You don't overcome the horsemen by overpaying, but the opposite is also true. You don't overcome the horsemen by underpaying, either.

Suppose someone is having their bathroom remodeled, and they are having a new tub installed. When it comes to hiring the plumber for the job, they decide to go with the company that would do the installation at the lowest cost. Everything goes smoothly. The tub is installed, and they couldn't be happier with the result and the look of their new bathroom.

Several years down the road, the same person is looking to move and sell the house. They believe they have found a buyer, and they are going through the inspection process. As fate would have it, when the inspector conducts a moisture test, he finds moisture in the wall on the other side of the tub. It turns out that when the plumber installed the bathtub, the overflow drain wasn't hooked up correctly, and water had been leaking into the wall for years.

Water damage is clearly visible inside the closet behind the tub. It was never noticed because of the stuff shoved into the closet. A mold test is done, and mold is growing inside the wall. The wall is opened up, and there is so much corrosion it is a sheer miracle there hasn't been an electrical fire.

Now our homeowner has a choice. They can reduce the price they are selling the home for, or they can pay to have the repairs done. Either solution is going to cost potentially thousands of dollars more than having the job done right from the beginning.

This same situation can exist no matter what type of professional you decide to use in life. If you need lifesaving surgery, are you out there looking for a doctor who can perform the surgery for the cheapest price? I sure hope not.

Does that mean you need to find the most expensive surgeon? No. You just need to find the one who can do the job right. The same goes for the plumber. Just because someone costs more doesn't mean they are better, but often, you get what you pay for.

If you find the cheapest tax preparer to file your taxes, you might think everything is going fine until you are audited by the IRS. If you hire the cheapest attorney, you might think everything is perfectly in place until you end up having that long-term care need, or you pass away, and your estate is a mess and subject to taxes that could have been avoided. If you hire the cheapest financial advisor, everything could be going exactly as planned until the first market decline. Those are just examples of things that could go wrong.

Possibly more detrimental than things going wrong is the opportunity cost of not getting the right advice. For instance, a tax preparer who costs more might potentially save you more on taxes. An attorney charging a higher rate could possibly help you protect more of your assets. Similarly, a financial advisor with a higher fee might help grow your assets more efficiently. While higher costs do not guarantee better results, they can reflect the value of experience and expertise. In all those cases, the more expensive option is clearly the better option, but that is harder to see. It's easier to notice when something goes wrong. It is harder to recognize what you missed out on and never had to begin with. That is opportunity cost.

I'm not advocating that you hire the most expensive professionals you can find. That clearly is not a good financial decision and not how you overcome the horsemen. I am advocating that you balance the cost you are paying with the value you are receiving. Fees are only an issue in the absence of value.

Ensure you are getting the advice you deserve for the fee you are paying. If you are going to pay your tax preparer an extra $500, are they helping you be proactive with tax planning throughout the year so that when you file your taxes, you can have the confidence in knowing that you are paying the least amount possible? If you pay the attorney an extra $150 an hour, are they giving you recommendations that you had never considered, helping you achieve your goals more efficiently and effectively? Suppose you pay your financial advisor an extra 0.25 percent. Are they looking at your full financial picture and creating a plan that optimizes your tax efficiency? Are they helping you make sure that your risk is aligned with your goals, educating you on new opportunities, and creating strategies to help ensure those you care for the most are well taken care of after you're gone? These are the questions I believe every family should be asking.

Overcoming the horsemen is no easy task. It takes looking at all the angles and having a plan. That's our last stop as we head to the conclusion of our story.

Chapter Eighteen

Taming The Four Horsemen With The 3D Retirement Map

My first child, Silas Lee Ford, was born on December 4, 2020. If you have children, maybe you felt like I did when you held that newborn baby for the first time. I've never felt more excited and driven about something or about someone in my entire life. I also remember a fleeting question to myself, "Who decided it was a good idea to trust me with a baby?"

I'll never forget that first night in the hospital when the joys of becoming a new father quickly dissipated when every single monitor hooked to my wife started blaring. She was experiencing a rare autoimmune disorder due to the trauma of childbirth. The following months were met with countless emergency room visits and hospitalizations. We faced years of having more questions than answers. We visited doctor after doctor and still had no answers. It felt like we were just being passed along, wandering aimlessly and getting nowhere.

We felt overwhelmed, lost, and confused. We were worried something was being overlooked, that we were missing something. We didn't know what we didn't know. Maybe most of all, we felt frustrated as we saw other families doing things with their children as a family that we simply couldn't do.

Finally, when going through another sleepless night, my wife and I stumbled upon a medical practice in Lake Nona, a small city outside of Orlando. At first, we had even more questions. Could we trust these people? After all, we just found them on the internet. How would they be different from anyone else? Could we finally get some answers?

After our first consultation, we had renewed hope. We met with a specialist and his team. We were asked questions we had never been asked before, given explanations we had never been given, and felt a real sense of care and urgency like our situation mattered.

Finally, we had found someone with a solution. My wife went through more testing than I ever knew was possible. That testing provided more answers. We were getting to the root cause. Those answers, those discoveries, were worked into a road map, an actual, actionable plan that we could pursue. For the first time in this journey, we had direction. We knew the possibilities. We had a clearer picture of the future. Most of all, we gained some peace of mind.

We followed that map to recovery. When we hit bumps in the road, that map equipped us with the knowledge of what to do to overcome the hurdles and get back on track.

You may have picked up this book feeling the same way about retirement as my wife and I felt early on in her medical journey. You feel like you have more questions than answers.

Do I have enough saved? Where will my money come from when I'm retired? If something happens to me, will my loved ones be OK? You're worried that you're missing something or that what you don't know you don't know will end up hurting you. Hopefully, some light has been shed on some of those questions as you've read the previous pages.

Maybe you look around at friends, colleagues, family members, and they seem to have the retirement thing all figured out. They know exactly where they're going, but you feel like you are wandering around, not knowing exactly what you need to do. You're a little lost, a little confused, a little overwhelmed, and you wish you had a plan, a map you could follow.

Building that map is what my company and my team specialize in. We help families identify the key components that are non-negotiable and must be included in your map for retirement. What do you need to get right so you can have the confidence to know that your money will last as long as you? You want to know that if something happens to you, your family will be OK. If there is a bump in the road, an unexpected twist or turn, you can navigate around it. You don't want to miss out on the retirement you dreamed about. I believe you deserve a great retirement.

That's why over the last forty years, our team has helped thousands of families, just like you, build the map they need to help them feel confident in their retirement.

For us, that map is called the 3D retirement map. That is the process of making sure families are equipped with the right map for mitigating the horsemen. You don't successfully mitigate the horsemen by running into battle without a plan and a strategy. The 3D retirement map is a plan designed to help you succeed.

The term "3D" is really a play on words. Our process starts with our discover peace of mind visit. This is our initial visit, where we begin to answer your family's basic questions and identify their needs, their goals, and their blind spots. We ask questions about when you want to retire. What do you hope to achieve? What are your goals? What's on your bucket list? What do you enjoy? What are your hobbies? What does money mean to you? Where do you want the money to go? Do you have a plan for how you are going to minimize taxes? How concerned are you about the market and experiencing losses? How much do you hope to gain? The list goes on.

Once we discover who you are and what you value most, we move on to the design phase. The is the second *D* in the 3D process. This is where our team of cartographers (map builders) goes to work building the plan based on your need, your concerns, and your goals. This plan will equip you with strategies designed to help you overcome the horsemen. We design a plan for Social Security, a pension, investments, taxes, healthcare, legacy, and estate.

When that is completed, we move to delivery. This is the third *D* in our process and the second visit we have with your family. During this visit, we will deliver the findings. We have a conversation about how to help maximize Social Security, optimize your investments, potentially decrease taxes, cover healthcare, and account for your last wishes.

Discover, design, and deliver: The three *D*'s of the 3D retirement map are just the beginning. We also call this a 3D map because we all live in three dimensions. Life is not flat and two-dimensional. There are six sides to a three-dimensional cube, and thus, the three more *D*'s in the process.

After delivery comes deploy. What good is a map if it is never put to use? We help families deploy their map to help mitigate the horsemen by acting as their personal guide on their quest, which continues with the next phase in the process.

Development is the next step in the process. There is no such thing as a one-and-done 3D retirement map. You need a plan that can adapt and evolve as life unfolds. You need a map that can be developed over time to help meet those additional needs. Development visits are those ongoing points of contact we have with families. These strategy and tactical visits help adapt your map to help you keep up with every changing landscape of your life. Our team is there to help families continually adjust their maps to keep them on the right path by helping them make decisions, manage their assets, and educate them on the changing landscape. That way, they can do the things they want to do, like travel and spend time with loved ones, and not worry about money.

Last but certainly not least are our destiny visits. It can be difficult to talk about, but one day, all of us are going to leave this Earth. Destiny visits are where we encourage families to bring in their loved ones to discuss their goals. It's completely optional, but many families have found it helpful to share their goals while they are still here. It's your money. The final vote is always with you. Otherwise, destiny visits happen with beneficiaries once it is time to transition assets, to help make sure everything is done following the rules in the most tax-efficient manner.

Discover, design, deliver, deploy, develop, and destiny—those are the six sides to the 3D retirement map. No map is completed without completing all six sides.

Having a map changed my family's life. I told you my first child, Silas Lee Ford, was born on December 4, 2020. My second child, something I thought I might never get to say, was born on April 6, 2023. Her name is Noa Jean Ford. My wife and I now have two beautiful children with hopefully more to come. Without our map, we wouldn't have gotten here. This would not have been possible without the guidance of the doctor who continually oversees my wife's recovery, helps us make the right decisions at the right time, and adjusts the map as needed. Our experience is why I encourage you to find a guide for your financial future, someone who can help you navigate around those twists and turns.

Conservative Financial Solutions exists to help families build the map they need for their retirement, walk alongside them to help them overcome obstacles, manage the assets, and feel confident their last wishes will be fulfilled when the time comes. It's what we love to do. It's what we're built to do. If you are interested in our services, we would love to hear from you.

CONSERVATIVE
FINANCIAL SOLUTIONS

Phone: (800) 368-9449
Email: info@conservativefinancialsolutions.com
Website: conservativefinancialsolutions.com

Acknowledgments

The hardest part about thanking everyone who helped me with this book is the fear of leaving someone out, but I'll do my best. I'll start by thanking my mother and father. As I mentioned before, my father started Conservative Financial Solutions LLC. I wouldn't be here without him, but my father wouldn't have been able to do what he did without my mother. While my father was building the firm, my mother did everything else to run the house and family. They taught me the power of teamwork and sticking things out even when they are hard.

I want to thank my brother Austin who is my co-CEO and the rest of the team at Conservative Financial Solutions LLC who took on extra work to create the capacity to write this book. I'm truly blessed to have a brother in the business. I wouldn't want to do it without him, and we have the best team anyone could ask for.

I want to thank the thousands of families who have entrusted us to help them along their retirement journey since the founding of Conservative Financial Solutions. Their trust and their stories are what made this book possible.

I want to thank my editor, Henry DeVries, and the entire team at Indie Books International. They kindly pushed me to stay on task and ensured we saw this thing through to publishing. They're true professionals, and their fingerprints are plentiful in this book.

Last but absolutely not least, I want to thank my family. I want to thank my son, Silas, and my daughter, Noa, who had to put up with Dad working long hours in his office at home to get this book done. I want to thank my beautiful wife, Brittany. None of this would be possible without her. She is the one who keeps everything at home running smoothly, and her support is what gives me the confidence to consistently strive to accomplish new things. I love you.

ABOUT THE AUTHOR

Passionate about helping others be their best, Spencer Ford has built his career on helping clients build more stable retirements. He holds a bachelor of arts in biblical studies and a master of arts in counseling from Cincinnati Christian University. This passion for helping others led him to Conservative Financial Solutions LLC.

Spencer holds an executive certificate in financial planning from The Ohio State University, has completed extensive training, and has met rigorous ethical experience requirements in order to obtain his Certified Financial Planner (CFP) professional designation. He has also passed the Series 7 exam—the General Securities Representative Qualification Examination—and the Series 63 and 65 exams—the North American Securities Administrators Association Investment Advisers Law Examination. Spencer is a licensed insurance agent in multiple states.

In his spare time, Spencer serves his community as a member of the local chamber of commerce. He enjoys volunteering at his church, flying, but most of all spending time with his family.

WORKS CITED AND AUTHOR'S NOTES

1   Michael McLeod, "The History of Retirement," Fiduciary Group, February 26, 2021, https://www.tfginvest.com/insights/the-history-of-retirement.

2   Bruce W. Frier, "Demography," in *The Cambridge Ancient History*, eds. Alan K. Bowman, Peter Garnsey, and Dominic Rathbone, vol. 11, *The High Empire*, A.D. 70–192, 2nd ed. (Cambridge University Press, 2000).

3   "Otto von Bismarck," History.com, updated June 7, 2019, https://www.history.com/topics/european-history/otto-von-bismarck.

4   McLeod, "History of Retirement."

5   "How Has Life Expectancy Changed Over Time?" British Office for National Statistics, September 9, 2015, https://www.ons.gov.uk/peoplepopulationandcommunity/birthsdeathsandmarriages/lifeexpectancies/articles/howhaslifeexpectancychangedovertime/2015-09-09.

6   Saloni Dattani, Lucas Rodés-Guirao, Hannah Ritchie, Esteban Ortiz-Ospina, and Max Roser, "Life Expectancy," Our World in Data, accessed November 4, 2024, https://ourworldindata.org/life-expectancy.

7   "Actuarial Life Table," Social Security Administration, 2021, accessed November 27, 2024, https://www.ssa.gov/oact/STATS/table4c6.html.

8   Greenwood and Associates, "Longevity Perceptions and Drivers: How Americans View Life Expectancy," Society of Actuaries, January 2020, https://www.soa.org/globalassets/assets/files/resources/research-report/2020/longevity-perceptions-drivers.pdf.

9   "Actuarial Life Table," Social Security Administration, 2021.

10 "Society of Actuaries (SOA) Age Wise Longevity Infographic Series," Society of Actuaries, accessed November 4, 2024, https://www.soa.org/research/age-wise/.

11 Maurie Backman. "1-in-2 working Americans underestimate their life expectancy by 5-plus years, resulting in skewed savings goals," Yahoo! Finance, September 26, 2024, https://finance.yahoo.com/news/1-2-working-americans-underestimate-110500118.html?guccounter=1.

12 "America's Gandhi: Martin Luther King Jr.," *Time*, January 3, 1964, https://time.com/sixty-two58531/martin-luther-king-jr-time-cover-1964/.

13   Liz Weston, "Will You Really Run Out of Money in Retirement?" NerdWallet, March 25, 2021, https://www.nerdwallet.com/article/finance/will-you-really-run-out-of-money-in-retirement.

14   "Outliving Your Money Feared More than Death," Allianz news release, June 17, 2010, https://www.allianzlife.com/~/Media/Files/Allianz/Documents/Reclaiming-The-Future/Rtf_6_17_2010.Pdf.

15 "Historical Background and Development of Social Security," Social Security Administration, accessed November 4, 2024, https://www.ssa.gov/history/briefhistory3.html.

16 "Cohort Life Expectancy," Social Security Administration, accessed November 27, 2024, https://www.ssa.gov/oact/tr/2012/lr5a4.html#.

17 "Actuarial Life Table," Social Security Administration, 2021.

18 Kat Tretina, "The Average Age of Retirement in the U.S.," *Forbes Advisor*, updated January 26, 2024, https://www.forbes.com/advisor/retirement/average-retirement-age/.

19 "Milton Friedman Speaks: Money and Inflation (B1230)—Full Video," lecture given at San Diego, California, 1 hr., 26 min., 3 sec., 1978, posted March 21, 2016, by Free to Choose Network, YouTube, https://www.youtube.com/watch?v=B_nGEj8wIP0&t=341s.

20 "1933: FDR Suspends the Gold Standard for U.S. Currency," This Day in History, History.com, accessed November 4, 2024, https://www.history.com/this-day-in-history/fdr-takes-united-states-off-gold-standard.

21 Nick Lioudis, "What Is the Gold Standard? History and Collapse," Investopedia, updated October 14, 2024, https://www.investopedia.com/ask/answers/09/gold-standard.asp.

22 "Inflation Rates in the United States of America," Worlddata.info, accessed July 13, 2024, https://www.worlddata.info/america/usa/inflation-rates.php.

23 Federal Reserve Reform Act of 1977, Pub. L. No. 111-148, 91 Stat. 1387 (1977) https://www.congress.gov/95/statute/STATUTE-91/STATUTE-91-Pg1387.pdf.

24 "Forum: Gold From The Gorbals," *New Scientist*, June 29, 1996, https://www.newscientist.com/article/mg15020366-000-forum-gold-from-the-gorbals/.

25 Congressional Budget Office. "Monthly Budget Review: Summary for Fiscal Year 2024," https://www.cbo.gov/publication/60843/html#:~:text=Outlays%20in%20fiscal%20year%202024,year%20average%20of%2021.1%20percent.&text=n.a.,-n.a.

26 "How to Cure Inflation," Free To Choose Network 1980, accessed November 20, 2024, https://www.freetochoosenetwork.org/programs/free_to_choose/index_80.php?id=how_to_cure_inflation.

27 "Milton Friedman Speaks," Free To Choose Network, March 21, 2016, https://www.bing.com/videos/riverview/relatedvideo?&q=%E2%80%9CMilton+Friedman+Speaks%2c%E2%80%9D+Free+To+Choose+Network&qpvt.

28 Madeline Coggins, "'Home Alone' Fans Shocked by Almost 250 Percent Increase in Grocery Prices Since Iconic Shopping Trip," Fox News, December 8, 2023, https://www.foxnews.com/media/home-alone-fans-shocked-250-percent-increase-grocery-prices-iconic-shopping-trip.

29 "Monetary Policy: What Are Its Goals? How Does It Work?" Board of Governors of the Federal Reserve System, last updated July 29, 2021, https://www.federalreserve.gov/monetarypolicy/monetary-policy-what-are-its-goals-how-does-it-work.htm.

30 "Consumer Price Index, 1913–," Federal Reserve Bank of Minneapolis, accessed November 5, 2024, https://www.minneapolisfed.org/about-us/monetary-policy/inflation-calculator/consumer-price-index-1913-.

31 "Food Inflation in the United States, 1968-2024," US Inflation Calculator, accessed November 20, 2024, https://www.usinflationcalculator.com/inflation/food-inflation-in-the-united-states/.

32 Rob McClelland, "Differences Between The Traditional CPI And The Chained CPI," CBO Blog, Congressional Budget Office, April 19, 2013, https://www.cbo.gov/publication/44088.

33 Julia Kagan, "What Is Bracket Creep?" Investopedia, updated October 30, 2024, https://www.investopedia.com/terms/b/bracketcreep.asp.

34 "United States Inflation Rate," Summary, 3Y, Trading Economics, accessed November 5, 2024, https://tradingeconomics.com/united-states/inflation-cpi.

35 Sarah Foster, "2022 Tax Brackets," Bankrate, November 13, 2023, https://www.bankrate.com/taxes/2022-tax-bracket-rates/ and "2021 Tax Brackets," Bankrate, January 17, 2023, https://www.bankrate.com/taxes/2021-tax-bracket-rates/.

36 Retirement Learning Center, "The Golden Age of Pensions: Another Fairy Tale," Retirement Learning Center, June 19, 2017, https://retirementlc.com/resources/the-golden-age-of-pensions-another-fairy-tale/.

37 James McWhinney, "The Demise Of The Defined-Benefit Plan and What Replaced It," Investopedia, updated May 12, 2024, https://www.investopedia.com/articles/retirement/06/demiseofdbplan.asp.

38 "A Summary of the 2024 Reports," Social Security Administration, accessed November 20, 2024, https://www.ssa.gov/oact/TRSUM/.

39 Alex J. Pollock, "Would You Take 77 Cents for Every Dollar Social Security Owes You?," American Enterprise Institute, July 8, 2015, https://www.aei.org/articles/would-you-take-77-cents-for-every-dollar-social-security-owes-you/.

40 "Policy Basics: Top Ten Facts about Social Security," Center on Budget and Policy Priorities, updated May 31, 2024, https://www.

cbpp.org/research/social-security/top-ten-facts-about-social-security.

41 Mary Johnson, "2022 Loss of Social Security Buying Power Study," Senior Citizens League, May 2022, https://seniorsleague.org/assets/2022-Loss-of-Buying-Power-Report.pdf.

42 Lorie Konish, "Another Record-High Social Security Cost-of-Living Adjustment In 2023 Could Put More Money into Retirees' Wallets, Impact Program's Funds," CNBC, updated June 6, 2022, https://www.cnbc.com/2022/06/06/social-security-cost-of-living-adjustment-in-2023-may-be-a-record-high.html.

43 Carroll Doherty and Jocelyn Kiley, "2. The Changing Composition Of The Electorate and Partisan Coalitions," *In Changing U.S. Electorate, Race and Education Remain Stark Dividing Lines*, Pew Research Center, June 2, 2020, https://www.pewresearch.org/politics/2020/06/02/the-changing-composition-of-the-electorate-and-partisan-coalitions/.

44 "Social Security Insolvency Projection Looking Better, But Still A Problem," FEDweek, June 14, 2022, https://www.fedweek.com/retirement-benefits/social-security-insolvency-projection-looking-better-but-still-a-problem/.

45 Kyle Burkhalter and Karen Rose, "Replacement Rates for Hypothetical Retired Workers," Actuarial Note Number 2024.9, Office of the Chief Actuary, Social Security Administration, May 2024, https://www.ssa.gov/OACT/NOTES/ran9/an2024-9.pdf.

46 Social Security Administration. 2025. "Retirement Benefits" https://www.ssa.gov/pubs/EN-05-10035.pdf.

47 "Cost-Of-Living Adjustments," Social Security Administration, accessed November 5, 2024, https://www.ssa.gov/OACT/COLA/colaseries.html.

48 "Almost All Americans Take Social Security at the Wrong Time, Study Says," CBS News, updated June 28, 2019, https://www.cbsnews.com/news/study-says-retirees-lose-more-than-100k-by-claiming-social-security-at-the-wrong-time/.

49 Katie Brockman, The Motley Fool, "Social Security: Research Shows This Age is the Best to Take Benefits—But There is a Big Caveat," Yahoo Finance, February 25, 2024, https://finance.yahoo.com/news/social-security-research-shows-age-150000738.html.

50 This is a hypothetical example provided for illustrative purposes only. It does not represent a real-life scenario and should not be construed as advice designed to meet the particular needs of an individual's situation. This is true for all hypothetical examples in the book.

51 James Royal, PhD., "When do Most Americans take Social Security?" Bankrate, February 21, 2024, https://www.bankrate.com/retirement/when-do-most-americans-take-social-security/.

52 Kat Tretina, "The Average Age Of Retirement In The U.S.," *Forbes Advisor*, updated January 26, 2024, https://www.forbes.com/advisor/retirement/average-retirement-age/.

53 Peter Gratton, "What Is a Pension? Types of Plans and Taxation," Investopedia, updated August 7, 2024, https://www.investopedia.com/terms/p/pensionplan.asp.

54 "What You Should Know About Your Retirement Plan," Employee Benefits Security Administration, United States Department of Labor, p. 3, September 2021, https://www.dol.gov/sites/dolgov/files/EBSA/about-ebsa/our-activities/resource-center/publications/what-you-should-know-about-your-retirement-plan.pdf.

55 "Cash Balance Pension Plans," Employee Benefits Security Administration, United States Department of Labor, January 2014, https://www.dol.gov/sites/dolgov/files/ebsa/about-ebsa/our-activities/resource-center/faqs/cash-balance-pension-plans-consumer.pdf.

56 "Annual Funding Notice for Defined Benefit Pension Plans," Pension Benefit Guaranty Corporation, accessed November 25, 2024, https://www.pbgc.gov/annual-funding-notice.

57 "How PBGC Operates," Pension Benefit Guaranty Corporation, last updated November 15, 2022, https://www.pbgc.gov/about/how-pbgc-operates, and "Who We Are," Pension Benefit Guaranty Corporation, last updated November 17, 2023, https://www.pbgc.gov/about/who-we-are.

58 Pension Benefit Guaranty Corporation. 2024. "2024 Annual Report" www.pbgc.gov/sites/default/files/documents/pbgc-annual-report-2024.pdf.

59 "FAQs: Plan Funding," Pension Benefit Guaranty Corporation, last updated February 26, 2021, https://www.pbgc.gov/about/faq/pg/planfundingfaq.

60 "Annual Report 2021," Pension Benefit Guaranty Corporation, 2021, www.pbgc.gov/sites/default/files/documents/pbgc-annual-report-2021.pdf#:~:text=For%20the%20first%20time%20in%20almost%20twenty,a%20positive%20net%20position%20at%20fiscal%20year%2Dend.&text=PBGC's%20Single%2DEmployer%20Program%20remains%20financially%20healthy%20with,FY%202020%2C%20an%20improvement%20of%20$15.4%20billion.

61 "Questions and Answers for Participants in the Sears Holdings Corporation Pension Plans," Pension Benefit Guaranty Corporation, last updated April 15, 2024. https://www.pbgc.gov/Questions-and-Answers-for-Sears-Participants.

62 Chris Isidore, "What's Killing Sears? Its Own Retirees, the CEO Says," CNN Business, September 14, 2018, https://money.cnn.com/2018/09/14/news/companies/sears-pension-retirees/index.html.

63 "GE Announces US Pension Plan Actions," BusinessWire.com, October 7, 2019, https://www.businesswire.com/news/home/20191007005406/en/GE-Announces-U.S.-Pension-Plan-Actions.

64 "Multiemployer Insurance Program Facts," Pension Benefit Guaranty Corporation, last updated August 13, 2021, https://www.pbgc.gov/about/factsheets/page/multi-facts.

65 "Projections Report," Pension Benefit Guaranty Corporation, last updated August 22, 2024. https://www.pbgc.gov/about/projections-report.

66 "Overview of Multiemployer Pension System Issues," American Academy of Actuaries, June 2017, https://www.actuary.org/content/overview-multiemployer-pension-system-issues.

67 Michael Katz, "UK Corporate Pensions' Deficit More than Doubles in December," Chief Investment Officer, January 7, 2019, https://www.ai-cio.com/news/uk-corporate-pensions-deficit-doubles-december/.

68 "Critical Status, Critical and Declining Status, Endangered Status, WRERA Status, and ARP Freeze Election Notices," DOL.gov,

accessed November 25, 2024, https://www.dol.gov/agencies/ebsa/about-ebsa/our-activities/public-disclosure/critical-status-notices.

69 Justin Alex and Mary Grace Richardson, "Ninth Circuit Agrees with Third Circuit that 'Highest Contribution Rate' for Withdrawal Liability Payment Calculations Excludes PPA Surcharges," Employee Benefits & Executive Compensation Blog, Proskauer, February 17, 2022, https://www.erisapracticecenter.com/2022/02/ninth-circuit-agrees-with-third-circuit-that-highest-contribution-rate-for-withdrawal-liability-payment-calculations-excludes-ppa-surcharges/.

70 "Overview of Multiemployer," American Academy of Actuaries. accessed May 14, 2025, https://www.actuary.org/content/overview-multiemployer-pension-system-issues.

71 Trina Paul, "Pensions Got a Boost From Strong Markets in 2024, But They're Still In Trouble," Investopedia, https://www.investopedia.com/pensions-got-a-boost-from-strong-markets-in-2024-but-theyre-still-in-trouble-8771111.

72 "Maximum Monthly Guarantee Tables," Pension Benefit Guaranty Corporation, last updated October 17, 2023, https://www.pbgc.gov/wr/benefits/guaranteed-benefits/maximum-guarantee.

73 "Guaranteed Benefits," Pension Benefit Guaranty Corporation, last updated May 14, 2021, https://www.pbgc.gov/wr/benefits/guaranteed-benefits#:~:text=Benefits.

74 "Multiemployer Benefit Guarantees," Pension Benefit Guaranty Corporation, last updated March 2, 2021, https://www.pbgc.gov/prac/multiemployer/multiemployer-benefit-guarantees.

75 "Multiemployer Benefit Guarantees," Pension Benefit Guaranty Corporation.

76 Maurie Backman. "1-in-2 working Americans underestimate their life expectancy by 5-plus years, resulting in skewed savings goals," Yahoo! Finance, September 26, 2024, https://finance.yahoo.com/news/1-2-working-americans-underestimate-110500118.html.

77 Kathleen Elkins, "A Brief History Of The 401(k), Which Changed How Americans Retire," CNBC, updated January 5, 2017, https://www.cnbc.com/2017/01/04/a-brief-history-of-the-401k-which-changed-how-americans-retire.html.

78 Elkins, "A Brief History."

79 Roth distributions are tax-free after age 59-1/2 and the account has been open for at least five years.

80 "How Much Do I Need to Retire?" Fidelity, August 21, 2024, https://www.fidelity.com/viewpoints/retirement/how-much-do-i-need-to-retire.

81 Glenn Ruffenach, "Is Your Adviser Still Right For Your Retirement?" Market Watch, Last Updated May 25, 2011, http://www.marketwatch.com/story/is-your-adviser-still-right-for-your-retirement-1304621779712.

82 "S&P 500 Total Returns by Year," Slickcharts, accessed November 5, 2024, https://www.slickcharts.com/sp500/returns.

83 Gerald P. Dwyer, "Stock Prices in the Financial Crisis," Federal Reserve Bank of Atlanta, September 2009, https://www.atlantafed.org/cenfis/publications/notesfromthevault/0909.

84 "S&P 500," Slickcharts.

85 "Nasdaq 100 Returns," Slickcharts, accessed November 5, 2024, https://www.slickcharts.com/nasdaq100/returns.

86 Sean Ross, "Has Real Estate or the Stock Market Performed Better Historically?" Investopedia, December 2024, https://www.investopedia.com/ask/answers/052015/which-has-performed-better-historically-stock-market-or-real-estate.asp.

87 Marcus Lu, "Ranked: The Top 6 Economies by Share of Global GDP (1980-2024)" Visual Capitalist, May 24, 2024, https://www.visualcapitalist.com/ranked-the-top-6-economies-by-share-of-global-gdp-1980-2024/.

88 "United States Population (LIVE)," Worldometer, accessed May 14, 2025, https://www.worldometers.info/world-population/us-population/#:~:text=the%20United%20States%20population%20is,98%20people%20per%20mi2.

89 "10-Year Treasury - Historical Annual Yield Data," Macrotrends, accessed November 5, 2024, https://www.macrotrends.net/2016/10-year-treasury-bond-rate-yield-chart.

90 "Consumer Price Index, 1913–," Federal Reserve Bank of Minneapolis, accessed May 14, 2025, https://www.minneapolisfed.org/about-us/monetary-policy/inflation-calculator/consumer-price-index-1913-.

91 "Annual Total Return (%) History," IShares Core U.S. Aggregate Bond ETF (AGG), Yahoo Finance, accessed July 15, 2024, https://finance.yahoo.com/quote/AGG/performance/.

92 "S&P 500," Slickcharts.

93 You will be subject to ordinary income taxes, and an additional 10% IRS penalty before age 59-1/2.

94 Troy Segal, "Are There Penalties for Withdrawing Money from Annuities?" Investopedia, January 24, 2025, https://www.investopedia.com/ask/answers/122414/are-there-penalties-withdrawing-monies-invested-annuities.asp#:~:text=In%20addition%20to%20penalties%20assessed,annuitant%20becomes%20disabled%20or%20dies.

95 "History of Innovation," Innovator, accessed November 6, 2024, https://www.innovatoretfs.com/timeline/.

96 "Buffer ETFs," Etf.com, accessed November 6, 2024, https://www.etf.com/topics/buffer.

97 Annuity guarantees are backed by the financial strength and claims-paying ability of the issuing company.

98 "S&P 500 Index - Historical Annual Data," Macrotrends, accessed November 6, 2024, https://www.macrotrends.net/2526/sp-500-historical-annual-returns.

99 These withdrawals are subject to income taxes and a 10 percent IRS penalty if you are under age 59-1/2.

100 "Why Pay Taxes When They Can Just Print Money?" BitcoinMemeHub.com, accessed November 22, 2024, https://x.com/BitcoinMemeHub/status/1289000939135803392.

101 Jessica Menton, "IRS Tax Season 2021: How Much Will You Pay in Taxes over a Lifetime?" USA Today, updated April 6, 2021, https://www.usatoday.com/story/money/2021/04/01/irs-tax-season-2021-how-much-do-you-pay-taxes-over-lifetime/7016671002/.

102 Cameron Huddleston, "Survey: 69% of Americans Have Less than $1,000 in Savings," Yahoo, December 16, 2019, https://www.yahoo.com/video/survey-69-americans-less-1-171927256.html.

103 "Sixteenth Amendment (1913)," Annenbergclassroom.org, accessed November 22, 2024, https://www.annenbergclassroom.org/resource/our-constitution/constitution-amendment-16.

104 "Historical U.S. Federal Individual Income Tax Rates &
Brackets, 1862–2021," Tax Foundation, August 24, 2021, https://
taxfoundation.org/historical-income-tax-rates-brackets/.

105 "Inflation Calculator," US Inflation Calculator, Coinnews
Media Group, accessed November 6, 2024, https://www.
usinflationcalculator.com/.

106 "Historical U.S. Federal Individual Income Tax," Tax Foundation,
August 24, 2021, https://taxfoundation.org/data/all/federal/
historical-income-tax-rates-brackets/.

107 Geoffrey Kollmann, "Social Security: Summary of Major Changes
in the Cash Benefits Program," Legislative History, Social Security
Administration, May 18, 2000, https://www.ssa.gov/history/
reports/crsleghist2.html.

108 "New Deal," History.com, updated March 28, 2023, https://www.
history.com/topics/great-depression/new-deal.

109 "National Debt," History.com, updated April 3, 2020, https://
www.history.com/topics/us-government/national-debt.

110 "US Government Debt: % of GDP," CEIC, accessed November 6,
2024, https://www.ceicdata.com/en/indicator/united-states/
government-debt--of-nominal-gdp.

111 "What is the national debt?" FiscalData, Treasury.gov, accessed
May 14, 2025, https://fiscaldata.treasury.gov/americas-finance-
guide/national-debt/.

112 "Final Monthly Treasury Statement," FiscalTreasury.gov, accessed
November 22, 2024, https://www.fiscal.treasury.gov/files/
reports-statements/mts/mts0924.pdf.

113 "Policy Basics, Introduction to the Federal Budget Process,"
CBBP.org, accessed November 22, 2024, https://www.cbpp.org/
research/federal-budget/introduction-to-the-federal-budget-
process#.

114 "How Much Revenue Has the U.S. Government Collected
this Year?" Fiscal Data, U.S. Treasury, accessed November 6,
2024, https://fiscaldata.treasury.gov/americas-finance-guide/
government-revenue/.

115 "How Much Has the U.S. Government Spent this Year?," Fiscal
Data, U.S. Treasury, accessed November 6, 2024, https://fiscaldata.
treasury.gov/americas-finance-guide/federal-spending/.

116 Garrett Watson, "Congressional Budget Office Shows 2017 Tax Law Reduced Tax Rates Across the Board in 2018," Tax Foundation, August 5, 2021, https://taxfoundation.org/congressional-budget-office-shows-2017-tax-law-reduced-tax-rates-across-board-2018/.

117 Justin Haskins, "IRS Data Proves Trump Tax Cuts Benefited Middle Working-Class Families Most," TheHill.com, December 4, 2021, https://thehill.com/opinion/finance/584190-irs-data-prove-trump-tax-cuts-benefited-middle-working-class-americans-most/.

118 "H.R.1994 - Setting Every Community Up For Retirement Enhancement Act of 2019," Congress.gov, accessed November 6, 2024, https://www.congress.gov/bill/116th-congress/house-bill/1994/text.

119 John Manganaro, "$35 Trillion In Retirement Savings Tells A Tale Of Two Economies," Planadvisor," March 18, 2021, https://www.planadviser.com/35-trillion-retirement-savings-tells-tale-two-economies/.

120 "Subtitle I _ Responsibly Funding Our Priorities, Section by Section," US House Ways And Means Committee, p. 10, accessed July 15, 2024, https://www.iraresources.com/hubfs/Ways&MeansBill-RetirementChanges-PAGE10.pdf.

121 If you're under the age of 59½, you'll also be assessed an additional 10% IRS penalty. Many employer-sponsored plans, like a 401(k) or 403(b), allow you to start taking money out penalty-free at age 55. You will still owe the tax, but you will not have a penalty.

122 Typically, following the rules means not taking withdrawals prior to age 59½ and having the account open for at least five years.

123 Greg Iacurci, "88% of Employers Offer a Roth 401(k)— Almost Twice as Many as a Decade Ago. Here's Who Stands to Benefit," CNBC, December 16, 2022, https://www.cnbc.com/2022/12/16/88percent-of-employers-offer-a-roth-401k-how-to-take-advantage.html.

124 "S&P 500," Slickcharts.

125 It's important to note that converting an employer plan account to a Roth IRA is a taxable event. Increased taxable income from the Roth IRA conversion may have several consequences, including (but not limited to) a need for additional tax withholding or estimated tax payments, the loss of certain tax deductions and credits, and higher taxes on Social Security benefits and higher

Medicare premiums. Be sure to consult with a qualified tax advisor before making any decisions regarding your IRA.

126 "S&P 500," Slickcharts.

127 "Give More, Tax-Free: Eligible IRA owners can donate up to $105,000 to charity in 2024," IR-2024-289, November 14, 2024, https://www.irs.gov/newsroom/give-more-tax-free-eligible-ira-owners-can-donate-up-to-105000-to-charity-in-2024.

128 Donor Advised Funds represent an irrevocable gift of assets from the donor to the fund. Contributions made to the fund are irrevocable and cannot be returned or used for any other individual or used for any purpose other than grant making to charities. The gift is not an investment or a security. When evaluating a contribution to the fund, carefully consider the terms and conditions, limitations, charges, and expenses. Depending on the tax filing status, DAF contributions may or may not be tax-deductible.

129 This hypothetical example is provided for illustrative purposes only; it does not represent a real-life scenario and should not be construed as advice designed to meet the particular needs of an individual's situation.

130 Kemberley Washington, CPA, and Sarah Foster. "2024 and 2025 tax brackets and current federal income tax rates," Bankrate, January 23, 2025, https://www.bankrate.com/taxes/tax-brackets/.

131 "2025 Medicare Parts A & B Premiums and Deductibles," CMS. gov, November 8, 2024, https://www.cms.gov/newsroom/fact-sheets/2025-medicare-parts-b-premiums-and-deductibles.

132 "The Long-Term Economic Effects of Some Alternative Budget Policies," Congressional Budget Office, May 19, 2008, p. 8, https://www.cbo.gov/sites/default/files/110th-congress-2007-2008/reports/05-19-longtermbudget_letter-to-ryan.pdf.

133 A ROTH Conversion is a taxable event that may not be right for everyone. Consult your tax advisor regarding your specific situation.

134 "Appendix C of the 1983 Greenspan Commission on Social Security Reform," Social Security Administration, accessed November 6, 2024, https://www.ssa.gov/history/reports/gspan5.html.

135 Anthony C. Kure, "The Golden Window for Strategic Retirement Tax Planning," Johnson Investment Counsel, November 17, 2021, https://www.johnsoninv.com/blog/retirement/the-golden-window-for-strategic-retirement-tax-planning.

136 Shameek Rakshit, Emma Wager, Paul Hughes-Cromwick, Cynthia Cox, and Krutika Amin, "How Does Medical Inflation Compare to Inflation in the Rest of the Economy?" Peterson-KFF Health System Tracker, updated August 2, 2024, https://www.healthsystemtracker.org/brief/how-does-medical-inflation-compare-to-inflation-in-the-rest-of-the-economy/.

137 "Fidelity Releases 2023 Retiree Health Care Cost Estimate: For the First Time in Nearly a Decade, Retirees See Relief As Estimate Stays Flat Year-Over-Year," Fidelity Newsroom, June 21, 2023, https://newsroom.fidelity.com/pressreleases/fidelity—releases-2023-retiree-healthcare-cost-estimate—for-the-first-time-in-nearly-a-decade—re/s/b826bf3a-29dc-477c-ad65-3ede88606d1c.

138 Nancy Ochieng, Jeannie Fuglesten Biniek, Karyn Schwartz, and Tricia Neuman, "Medicare-Covered Older Adults Are Satisfied with Their Coverage, Have Similar Access to Care as Privately-Insured Adults Ages 50 to 64, And Fewer Report Cost-Related Problems," Issues Brief, KFF, May 17, 2021, https://www.kff.org/report-section/medicare-covered-older-adults-are-satisfied-with-their-coverage-have-similar-access-to-care-as-privately-insured-adults-ages-50-to-64-issue-brief/.

139 "Quarter of Coverage," Social Security Administration, accessed November 6, 2024, https://www.ssa.gov/OACT/COLA/QC.html.

140 "2025 Medicare Parts A & B Premiums and Deductibles," CMS.gov, November 8, 2024, https://www.cms.gov/newsroom/fact-sheets/2025-medicare-parts-b-premiums-and-deductibles.

141 Alex Rosenberg, "What Is the Medicare 'Donut Hole,' Or Part D Coverage Gap?" NerdWallet, updated September 10, 2024, https://www.nerdwallet.com/article/insurance/medicare/medicare-donut-hole.

142 "2025 Medicare Parts A & B Premiums and Deductibles, " CMS.gov.

143 "Avoid Late Enrollment Penalties," Medicare, accessed November 6, 2024, https://www.medicare.gov/basics/costs/medicare-costs/avoid-penalties.

144 S. Srakocic, "Medicare Supplement Plans Comparison Chart," Healthline, October 16, 2024, https://www.healthline.com/health/medicare/medicare-supplement-plans-comparison-chart#benefit-chart.

145 "Why Exactly Is Plan F Being Phased Out?" Sams Hockaday And Associates, blog, accessed July 15, 2024, https://www.samshockaday.com/blog/why-exactly-is-plan-f-being-phased-out.

146 Christian Worstell, "What Is the Average Cost of Medicare Supplement Insurance?" MedicareSupplement.com, October 12, 2023, https://www.medicaresupplement.com/articles/average-cost-of-medicare-supplement-by-age/.

147 Gretchen Morgenson, "'Deny, Deny, Deny': By Rejecting Claims, Medicare Advantage Plans Threaten Rural Hospitals and Patients, Say CEOs," NBC News, October 31, 2023, https://www.nbcnews.com/health/rejecting-claims-medicare-advantage-rural-hospitals-rcna121012.

148 "Medicare Advantage Trial Period," Humana, accessed July 15, 2024, https://www.humana.com/medicare/medicare-resources/medicare-advantage-trial-period.

149 Dena Bunis, "Will Original Medicare Survive The Medicare Advantage Boom?," AARP, September 27, 2023, https://www.aarp.org/health/medicare-insurance/info-2023/will-original-medicare-survive-medicare-advantage.html.

150 Jakob Emerson, "Hospitals Are Dropping Medicare Advantage Plans Left and Right," Becker's Hospital CFO Report, December 14, 2023, https://www.beckershospitalreview.com/finance/hospitals-are-dropping-medicare-advantage-left-and-right.html.

151 Morgenson, "'Deny, Deny, Deny.'"

152 "When Should You Start Investing in Long-Term Care Insurance?" NCOA.org, August 5, 2024, https://www.ncoa.org/article/when-should-you-start-investing-in-long-term-care-insurance/.

153 "Cost of Care Survey," Genworth.com, accessed November 25, 2024, https://www.genworth.com/aging-and-you/finances/cost-of-care.

154 "Cost of Care Survey," Genworth.com.

155 Christine Benz, "100 Must Know Statistics About Long Term Care," March 29, 2023, https://www.morningstar.com/personal-finance/100-must-know-statistics-about-long-term-care-2023-edition.

156 "Medicaid's Community Spouse Resource Allowance (CSRA): Calculations & Limits," American Council on Aging, last updated January 09, 2024, https://www.medicaidplanningassistance.org/community-spouse-resource-allowance/.

157 "Understand Medicaid's Look-Back Period; Penalties, Exceptions & State Variances," Medical Planning Assistance, American Council on Aging, last updated January 26, 2024, https://www.medicaidplanningassistance.org/medicaid-look-back-period/.

158 Anne Kelly, Jessamyn Conell-Price, Kenneth Covinsky, et al., "Lengths of Stay for Older Adults Residing in Nursing Homes at the End of Life," August 24, 2010, https://pmc.ncbi.nlm.nih.gov/articles/PMC2945440/.

159 "Understand Medicaid's Look-Back Period; Penalties, Exceptions and State Variances," American Council on Aging, Last updated November 21, 2024, https://www.medicaidplanningassistance.org/medicaid-look-back-period/.

160 "Understanding Medicaid's Estate Recovery Program (MERP) and How to Protect The Home," American Council on Aging, Last Updated April 24, 2024, https://www.medicaidplanningassistance.org/medicaid-estate-recovery-program/.

161 Life insurance death benefits are typically tax-free to a properly named beneficiary. Life insurance agents do not provide tax or legal advice.

162 Tony Robbins et al., *Life Force: How New Breakthroughs in Precision Medicine Can Transform the Quality of Your Life & Those You Love* (Simon & Schuster, 2022).

163 Blake Farmer, "When Doctors Struggle with Suicide, Their Profession Often Fails Them," Shots, NPR, July 31, 2018, https://www.npr.org/sections/health-shots/2018/07/31/634217947/to-prevent-doctor-suicides-medical-industry-rethinks-how-doctors-work.

164 Peter Attia, MD, and Bill Gifford, *Outlive: The Science and Art of Longevity* (Harmony, 2023). Kindle edition.

165 Attia, *Outlive*, p. 10.

166 Attia, *Outlive*, pp. 16-17.

167 Christine Colacino, "Medicine in a Changing World," News & Research, Harvard Medical School, March 2, 2017, https://hms. harvard.edu/news/medicine-changing-world.

168 Linh Dang, Aparna Ananthasubramaniam, and Briana Mezuk, "Spotlight on the Challenges of Depression Following Retirement and Opportunities for Interventions," *Clinical Interventions* in Aging 17 (2022): 1037–56, https://doi.org/10.2147/CIA.S336301.

169 Julia Kagan, "Probate Court: Definition and What Goes through Probate," Investopedia, updated July 30, 2024, https://www. investopedia.com/terms/p/probate-court.asp.